TWAYNE'S WORLD AUTHORS SERIES
A Survey of the World's Literature

WEST INDIES

Robert McDowell, University of Texas at Arlington

EDITOR

The West Indian Novel

TWAS 592

THE WEST INDIAN NOVEL

By MICHAEL GILKES
University of the West Indies

TWAYNE PUBLISHERS
A DIVISION OF G. K. HALL & CO., BOSTON

Copyright © 1981 by G. K. Hall & Co.

Published in 1981 by Twayne Publishers,
A Division of G. K. Hall & Co.
All Rights Reserved

Printed on permanent/durable acid-free paper and bound
in the United States of America

First Printing

Library of Congress Cataloging in Publication Data

Gilkes, Michael.
The West Indian novel.

(Twayne's world authors series; TWAS 592. West Indies)
Bibliography: p. 164–67
Includes index.
1. West Indian fiction (English)—History and criticism.
I. Title.   II. Series: Twayne's world authors series; TWAS 592.
III. Series: Twayne's world authors series. West Indies.
PR9214.G5   823'.009'9729   81–973
ISBN 0–8057–6434–8   AACR2

Contents

About the Author

Michael Arthur Gilkes holds a first class B.A. honors Degree from the University of London and a doctorate from the University of Kent at Canterbury. Born in Guyana in 1933, he has taught at three universities: the University of Guyana, the University of Kent, and the Cave Hill (Barbados) Campus of the University of the West Indies.

He has already had published two books on West Indian fiction: *Wilson Harris and the Caribbean Novel* (Longman Caribbean 1975) was the first critical book published on the work of Wilson Harris, while *Racial Identity and the Individual Consciousness* (National History and Arts Council, Guyana 1974) was the fourth in the series of Edgar Mittelholzer memorial lectures delivered in Georgetown, Guyana.

As well as contributing many reviews and articles to various journals including the *Journal of Commonwealth Literature, Caribbean Quarterly,* and *World Literature Written in English* (WLWE), Dr. Gilkes has worked as scriptwriter and broadcaster for the Literature Programme of Guyana's "Broadcasts to Schools" Service. He is author of *Couvade* (Longman Caribbean 1974), a full length play commissioned and first performed for *Carifesta* 1972, where it was Guyana's entry in the Drama category. *Couvade* has since been performed by the Kenya National Theatre in Nairobi in 1974 and by the Keskidee Centre, Islington, London, in 1978.

More recently, Dr. Gilkes devised, produced, and directed a multimedia dramatization of Edward Brathwaite's *Mother Poem*, which was selected to be Barbados's gala performance at *Carifesta '79* in Havana, Cuba.

He is at present at work on a novel, a new play, and a handbook, "The Living Text," on the use of audio-visual methods in the teaching of literature.

Preface

Of all the hazards that accompany any attempt to produce a survey of a literary *genre* (in this case the relatively new one of "West Indian Fiction"), perhaps the most obvious are the dangers of overgeneralization and, at the other extreme, overconcentration. In attempting to keep the subject in focus for the viewer, one may decide to sacrifice "depth-of-field" for sharp detail, or vice versa. I have tried to avoid both dangers by using the double approach of general development *and* close critical analysis within a chronological framework. I have, however, thereby exposed myself to the charge of a certain deliberate (though, I hope, not arbitrary) shifting of the focus.

An introductory, "aerial" view of the development of the novel away from a colonial, Europe-oriented condition of "mimicry," toward a self-conscious, "West Indianizing" phase (Chapter 1) leads directly into a close, critical appraisal of specific works by De Lisser, Mendes, Mais, and Mittelholzer. This is followed by a general discussion of the major works of three later "exiles," Lamming, Naipaul, and St. Omer (Chapter 2) as an illustration of the way in which these writers reject, with both irony and compassion, the stereotype of "West Indian" character and society. Theirs is a search for the truth of personal experience and private sensibility.

The focus in Chapter 3 changes again to provide a detailed discussion of two important "classics" of childhood—Reid's *New Day* and Lamming's *In the Castle of My Skin*—as a way of observing the importance of the novel of "growing up" as a stage toward a genuinely indigenous reality: a *realized* "landscape of feeling."

Finally, Chapter 4 begins with a backward look at a much-neglected work which stands at the beginning of what is now a remarkable new direction in West Indian fiction. A detailed critical examination of W. H. Hudson's *Green Mansions* (1904) leads to the more general discussion of the innovative development of the ancient "journey motif," first noticeable in Hudson's strangely "shamanistic" novel. This new direction in West Indian writing is most clearly reflected (again, with a shift in focus) in the work of Denis Williams and Wilson Harris, the latter tending toward a view of the West Indies which embraces not only the wider concept, "Caribbean," but also the South American "magical reality" of a Carpentier or of a Márquez. With the work of Wilson Harris, the West Indian novel, while remaining rooted in a native sensibility, becomes capable of far wider associations and of a remarkable diversity of both form and meaning.

The book's most serious limitations come from the inevitable exigency of space—I have had, for example, to forego a discussion of the many fine works of short fiction which gave impetus to the novel's development—and from such subjective matters as selection, emphasis, and taste for which I am alone accountable, and for which I offer no apology. West Indian literature is now a literature in its own right, and its critics do not need to be either advocate or judge.

It is, however, difficult to ignore the irony of a Metropolitan acceptance existing alongside an equally and almost obdurate Metropolitan vagueness about the nature of the West Indian reality. Dr. Edward Baugh's valuable addition to the well-known Allen & Unwin series of Readings in Literary Criticism (*Critics on West Indian Literature*, 1978) reflects the Metropole's acceptance: a literature has surely "arrived" when there can be a book dealing with its critics. On the other hand, in *The Novel Today: 1967–1975*, published by Longmans in 1976, Ronald Hayman, albeit in a swift survey of the Commonwealth novel, can still refer to "the West Indies and British Guiana." Guyana, independent since 1966, is, like Surinam, *in* South America but *of* the West Indies. But then the growth and development of a "West Indian" reality has not been without its own peculiar ironies.

MICHAEL GILKES

University of the West Indies

Introduction

Even the term "West Indian" contains certain ironies. A misnomer to begin with—Columbus in 1492 thought he had discovered the fabled Indies of Marco Polo—it was first used to identify the *white* Creole plantation owners who had investments in the British colonies within and around the Caribbean Sea. In an eighteenth-century English play, the servants in a well-to-do London home are making preparations for the arrival of the hero, the "West Indian":

Housekeeper: Why, what a fuss does our good master put himself in about this West Indian! . . . Why if my Lord Mayor was expected, there couldn't be a greater to-do about him . . . had he been . . . a Christian Englishman there could not be more rout than there is about this Creolian, as they call 'em.

Servant: No matter for that; he's very rich, and that's sufficient. They say he has rum and sugar enough belonging to him, to make all the water in the Thames into punch. (Act I Scene iii of Richard Cumberland's *The West Indian*, 1771)

From such a background of the character of the "West Indian," little in the way of literary development could be expected; and John Stuart's sober commentary in his *An Account of Jamaica and Its Inhabitants* (1808) may be seen as the sociological background to, and explanation of, the later development of West Indian literature:

Literature is little cultivated in Jamaica. . . . The ardent thirst and eager pursuit of gain, by which so large a proportion of the people of this country are more or less actuated, is a passion naturally hostile to literary pursuits. (pp. 171, 173)

Literary reference to, or activity in, the West Indies tended, therefore, to be the result of occasional visits from articulate, well-bred outsiders,[1] the journals of literate plantation owners, or the well-meaning but condescending attempts to "rehabilitate" the degraded blacks by writers like Mrs. Aphra Benn and the Duke of Montagu.

9

The former, in *Oroonoko*, a short novel published in 1688, describes the black hero, a slave with a royal pedigree, in terms of an English courtier. The latter conducted an experiment to discover whether, "by proper cultivation and a regular course of tuition at school and the university, a Negro might not be found as capable of literature as a white person" (in Edward Long, *The History of Jamaica*, 1774).[2] The subject of the experiment, Francis Williams, carefully nourished on an English literary diet, duly produced a literate, if dull, Latin ode: "To Mr. Haldane upon his assuming the government of the island." It is the work of one who might be regarded as a literary house-Negro.

Even the clear-headed, often ironic prose of *The Interesting Narrative of the Life of Olaudah Equiano, or Gustavus Vassa the African, Written by Himself* (1789) reads like the journal of an outsider, an observer who is as much an alien to the West Indies as Mrs. Aphra Benn.

Edward Brathwaite, in his essay "Creative Literature of the British West Indies During the Period of Slavery" (*Savacou*, Jamaica, 1:1 [1970]), acknowledges that

given the origin and, in the case of the Native West Indians, the education of these writers, we cannot expect to find, during this period, "West Indian" writing as we understand the term today. (p. 47)

He claims, however, that there *was* some significant creative "Creole" writing, Creole to the extent that the writers "had intimate knowledge of and were in some way committed by experience and/or attachment to the West Indies" (p. 47). But this has the sound of special pleading, and Brathwaite admits that, of the sampling of novels he offers, only seven are worth considering as "written from direct West Indian experience" (p. 60), and only one, *Hamel, the Obeah Man*, offers something more than a record of certain aspects of West Indian slave society or a tract aimed at encouraging white pity and condescension toward the slaves.

Hamel, the Obeah Man is also a tract, but an antimissionary one, and since the author wanted to show that the "white magic" of the Christian missionaries was even more pernicious than the "black magic" of the natives, he is forced to make Hamel, a black man, the central character, and to portray him at some depth. Though Hamel, near the end of the book, delivers "what is probably the first Black Power speech in our history" (p. 71), Brathwaite concedes that the

book is "deeply race-conscious and colour-prejudiced" (p. 69), and
that it is remarkable only insofar as the author, in spite of his obvious
bias, is able to "enter into the imagination of at least a single slave"
(p. 72). It is not enough of a claim, however, to warrant the description "creative West Indian writing." The literature of the period of
slavery remains insignificant, proof almost of the obdurate philis-
tinism of the ruling class in the West Indies. The Jamaican "journals"
and "gazettes" of the time, as Kenneth Ramchand notes, indicated
that the interest in literature was not only slight, but "amateurish and
trifling in practice, and turned towards England in theory" (*The West
Indian Novel and Its Background.* London: Faber, 1970, p. 36).

Yet it was from Jamaica that a recognizably West Indian literature
first began to emerge. Thomas H. MacDermot ("Tom Redcam") published his *Becka's Buckra Baby* in Kingston in 1903 as the first novel
of a project called "The All-Jamaica Library." The foreword spoke of
an attempt to present, to a Jamaican public, a literary collection of
poetry, fiction, history and essays, all written by Jamaicans and "dealing directly with Jamaica and Jamaicans." The project, however, did
not go beyond five volumes and, although its objectives were admirable, a deliberate, if self-conscious, attempt to encourage a genuinely
'West Indian' literature, the novels themselves offer little more than
propaganda for a native "folk"-consciousness.

In the novels of Herbert G. De Lisser (1878–1944) one sees the
beginning of a genuine awareness of, if not an engagement with, the
realities of everyday West Indian life. De Lisser was a white Jamaican, quite well off financially, and a prominent member of his society.
At twenty-six he had risen from lowly proofreader to editor of the
newspaper the *Jamaica Gleaner,* a post he held for about forty years.
Strongly conservative in his tastes, and an Establishment figure, he
contributed humorous articles ("As I see the world; by H.G.D.") to
the newspaper and wrote novels as a literary hobby. Yet his first
novel, *Jane's Career* (London: Methuen & Co., 1914), shows surprising insight into the life of the Jamaican lower classes and is the first
noteworthy West Indian novel in which the central character is
black. De Lisser's other novels are mainly historical, bear little relationship to a contemporary West Indian locale, and reflect his increasingly reactionary attitude to political change: he was against
self-government for the colony and propounded his views in *Gleaner*
editorials. His novel *Revenge* (Jamaica, 1919), dealing with the
Morant Bay uprising in 1865, portrays the black patriot Paul Bogle
(leader of the uprising) as a near savage, suggests that George Wil-

liam Gordon (a sympathizer and member of the House of Assembly) was a "mulatto traitor," and sees Governor Eyre as a much-needed "voice of authority." [3]

Jane's Career is of special interest not only because it reflects the author's earlier and less prejudiced and reactionary political views, but also because it is a novel that deals with contemporary West Indian life at the grass-roots level.

But De Lisser, like "Tom Redcam," was a lone figure whose work did little to foster a genuine West Indian literature. So too was the black writer Claude McKay (1890–1948), who left his native Jamaica in 1912 for America and so became the first of a long line of West Indian émigré writers. McKay's sojourn in America coincided with the rise of Negro art and culture in Harlem (the "Harlem Renaissance" of 1920–1930) and Marcus Garvey's Back-to-Africa movement and Negro Improvement Organization. He found a climate, therefore, which offered him the chance of an audience he could never have hoped for in Jamaica. His first novel, *Home to Harlem* (New York: Harper and Brothers, 1928), sold more than 50,000 copies in the first year. But, as Eckhard Breitinger points out in his lecture on McKay ("In Search of an Audience . . ." published in *Commonwealth Writer Overseas*, Brussels: Didier, 1976), the Harlem Renaissance was itself part of "a faddish pro-Negro vogue of the Jazz age which made all Negro material a marketable commodity" (p. 175) and McKay's audience was "a predominantly white intellectual audience" (p. 175). His novels, like the poetry he had written and had published in America and the work he had done in England as a reporter for the *Workers Dreadnought* (the magazine edited by the suffragette leader Sylvia Pankhurst), were well received firstly because he was that rare thing, a literate Negro, and only secondly because of the merit of the work. McKay is essentially a poet of social and racial protest, and his novels tend to be extensions of this theme. *Home to Harlem*, like his second novel, *Banjo: A Story without a Plot* (New York: Harper and Brothers, 1929), is almost exclusively concerned with the predicament of the "displaced" black man in a white society. Both books, as Ramchand puts it, "[take] the form of a celebration of Negro qualities on the one hand, and attacks upon the civilized white world on the other" (*The West Indian Novel and Its Background*, p. 247).

Home to Harlem is episodic in form, the adventures on the road of its Picaroon hero Jacob Brown, who is black and proud of it. He is tall, brawny, and known to his friends as Jake. The story begins after the declaration of war by America on Germany in 1917. Jake has enlisted and is sailing for Brest with "a happy chocolate company." He doesn't take part in any fighting since that is reserved for the more fortunate whites. He then deserts and his travels begin. He visits Paris and London and then returns to Harlem, where the important and central episodes of the novel take place. The main point the book makes is that Harlem—the "nigger heaven"—contains genuinely alive, happy people in spite of its squalor, and Jake, as an unrepentant, self-confessed womanizer, spends most of the book looking (albeit sporadically) for his "lost brown," the girl he first sees in a boardinghouse of doubtful reputation. Jake is not so much a stereotyped Negro as his author's admission that such a stereotype exists, and he is likable, though not very bright. The most interesting character, a mouthpiece, one feels, for the author, is a character from Haiti, the Negro Jake befriends while he is working on a train. This is Ray, the educated character in the book. During a discussion in the section entitled "A practical Prank," Ray's remarks receive obvious authorial approval:

"Why not," asked Grant, "can't a Negro have fine feelings about life?"
"Yes," Ray replies, "but not the old false fine feelings that used to be monopolized by educated and cultivated people. We ought to get something new, we negroes." (pp. 242–43)

Earlier, Ray, the West Indian, is thinking about Haiti. Since, he argues to himself, he was conscious of being black and impotent, so, correspondingly

each marine down in Hayti must be conscious of being white and powerful. What a unique feeling of confidence about life the typical white youth of his age must have! (pp. 154–55)

Ray is a spokesman for the West Indian Negro point of view. He doesn't any longer feel condescendingly toward the African or the American blacks. Yet Jake is aware that "he possessed another language and literature that they knew not of" (p. 155). Ray, dreaming of becoming a writer someday, thinks of all his experience in literary terms, and if he is the potential Negro writer in the book, Jake, "nosing through life, a handsome hound, quick to snap up any tempting morsel of poisoned meat thrown carelessly on the pavement" (pp. 228–29), is the embodiment of the Negro soul attracted inevitably to life. It is almost as if Ray (literature) and Jake (life) together represent the twin poles of what McKay regards as the "wholeness" of experience and Harlem becomes symbolic of the emotional centrality, the instinct for life that McKay, at any rate, considers essentially Negro. A good deal is made of color, that is, the variety of darker shades that make up Harlem. " 'Harlem, Harlem,' thought Jake, 'where else could I have all this life but Harlem. Good old Harlem. Chocolate Harlem' " (p. 14). McKay makes much of the "chocolate" aspect of Harlem, but it is, perhaps, significant that things end happily for Jake only when he finds his "lost brown," the chestnut-colored girl. The implicit preference, at least for Jake, is a lighter shade of brown. The novel shows evidence of untidy organization. Many of the episodes are gratuitous and unrelated to a particular theme, and there are occasional signs of deliberately "sensational" writing. During a fight, for example, when Jake disarms Zeddy, one reads: "Jake aimed a swift kick at his elbow. The razor flew, spinning upward and fell chopping through a glass of gin on the pianola" (p. 52). There is also a character, presumably Jewish, who exploits the moneyed "golden browns" and is named, predictably, "Goldgraben." In spite of McKay's hasty writing and a frequently unconvincing use of dialect, the essential sense of ghetto life, the life of Harlem, comes through without condescension.

Even *Banana Bottom* (New York: Harper and Brothers, 1933), in spite of the large claims made for it,[4] reads like a case of special pleading for an indigenous, rooted Black Consciousness. Bita Plant, the novel's heroine, finds a place that is truly "home" by finding a "solution" (the inverted commas suggest themselves) to the familiar West Indian dichotomy: she is able to "prevent a Western education from separating her from . . . the soulfulness of her roots" (George E. Kent in "The Soulful Way of Claude McKay," *Black World* 20 [1970]: 48). *Banana Bottom* is an idealized "home," a folk-centered community in which the black or colored West Indian can live in harmony with himself and others; and it is the ideal that powers the work of most of the later writers. C. L. R. James's *Minty Alley* (1936), Roger Mais's barrack-yards, Mittelholzer's "Berkelhoost" (in *Shadows Move among Them*, 1952), John Hearne's "Cayuna," and George Lamming's "San Cristobal" are all later, more complex communities illustrating the West Indian's need to find a sense of belonging, of being truly West Indian.

It was in the 1930s, in Trinidad, that a literary "movement," a group of West Indian writers and thinkers, came together to create the nucleus for a genuine literature. The "little magazines" which these writers edited and published offered an outlet for their own talent and the talents of others. *Trinidad* was edited by Alfred H. Mendes and C. L. R. James, and *The Beacon* by Albert Gomes. *Trinidad* survived only two editions (Christmas 1929 and Easter 1930), but *The Beacon* ran from March 1931 to November 1933 through twenty-eight issues. What distinguishes these magazines, however, from the earlier, abortive "All Jamaica Library" of "Tom Redcam" is not only their nature as literary forums, but the fact that they encouraged an exchange of views between the writers and expanded the scope of their concerns. Gomes, Mendes, and James were themselves writers and met frequently to discuss ideas, listen to recorded music, and read their work to each other. As Reinhard W. Sander records in his anthology, *From Trinidad* (London: Hodder & Stoughton, 1978):

It is important to note that the group around *The Beacon*, although living in a remote colonial island, was well-informed about social and political activities not only in the British Empire, but also in the United States, Western Europe and the Soviet Union. (p. 4)

The short fiction which these writers encouraged and printed heralded the development of the West Indian novel of social realism. This was also the function of the related magazines *Bim* (published in Barbados from 1942 and now in its sixty-second edition) and *Kyk-Over-Al* (published in Guyana from 1945 to 1961). The West Indian novel may fairly be said to have grown out of the short fiction and poetry which these magazines encouraged. Most of the present-day writers began as contributors to *Bim* or *Kyk-Over-Al* or to both.

Alfred Mendes, in an interview with Reinhard Sander, is reported as having said that he deliberately, as a middle-class writer, went to live in a barrack-yard in Trinidad

to get the sort of jargon that they spoke—the vernacular, the idiom—
. . . and a lot of the incidents that appear in my second published novel, *Black Fauns*, were taken almost directly from my experience with the barrack-yarders. (Reinhard Sander, *From Trinidad*, p. 7)

C. L. R. James, too, was aware of the need for a "first-hand" experience of the yard dwellers in order to give authenticity to any writing about their kind of life. Referring to *Minty Alley* (1936) James said, in an interview: "I was about twenty-seven or twenty-eight at the time when I went to live in that household described in the novel" (*Kas-Kas*, Austin: University of Texas, 1972, p. 33). This study, therefore, begins with a consideration of the work of the early "pioneers" and with a detailed discussion of De Lisser's *Jane's Career* and C. L. R. James's *Minty Alley*.

Chronology

The following brief list of major (and some minor, but interesting) historical, social, political, and literary events in the Caribbean, Europe, and America is intended to convey something of the general movement of international trends against which the development of the West Indian novel may be seen. The list goes only as far as the 1930s, the period during which a distinctly "West Indian" fiction may be said to have its origins.

	Caribbean	Europe (esp. Britain)	America
1492		Columbus's first voyage of discovery to New World.	
1562	Hawkins initiates slave trade to W.I.		
1590		Sir Philip Sidney's Arcadia.	
1610–1611	Consolidation of Dutch in Guiana.		
1622–1632	English and French establish settlements in W.I. islands.		
1678–1684		Bunyan's Pilgrim's Progress.	
1680		Mrs. Aphra Benn's Oroonoko.	
1706			Birth of Benjamin Franklin.
1719		Defoe's Robinson Crusoe.	
1726		Swift's Gulliver's Travels.	

	Caribbean	Europe (esp. Britain)	America
1756–1763		Seven years' war between Britain and France.	
1759	Francis Williams's "Ode to Governor Haldane" (first known poem by a black West Indian).	Dr. Samuel Johnson's *Rasselas*.	
1760		Laurence Sterne's *Tristram Shandy*.	
1763	Slave rebellion in Dutch-held Guiana (led by Cuffy).		
1765		British Anti-Slavery Society founded.	
1776–1783			Declaration of Independence.
1783		*Treaty of Versailles* concluded. Britain cedes St. Lucia, Tobago, to France. France restores St. Kitts, Nevis, Montserrat, Grenada, Grenadines, and St. Vincent to Britain.	
1786			Birth of the legendary Davy Crockett.
1789		French Revolution.	James Fenimore Cooper born.
		The Interesting Narrative of the Life of Olaudah Equiano . . . (publ. in Britain).	
1794	Haitian revolution.		

Caribbean	Europe (esp. Britain)	America
1799		Charles Brockden Brown's *Arthur Mervyn*.
1805	Battle of Trafalgar. Nelson defeats French and Spanish fleets.	
1807	Bill for abolition of British slave trade passed in Parliament.	
1813	Jane Austen's *Pride and Prejudice*.	
1821		American Colonization Society settles liberated slaves in Africa (Liberia).
1823	The Demerara Slave Revolt (British Guiana).	
1826		James F. Cooper's *The Last of the Mohicans*.
1827	*Hamel the Obeah Man* (London).	
1831	Demerara, Essequibo, and Berbice become British Guiana.		Nat Turner's slave rebellion.
1833	British emancipation of slaves.	
1834		Matthew G. ("Monk") Lewis's *Journal of a West Indian Proprietor*. Michael Scott's *Tom Cringle's Log* (Edin-	

	Caribbean	Europe (esp. Britain)	America
		burgh) publ. in Paris in 1836.	
1838	Indian indentured labor imported to British West Indies.		
1839		Lady Nugent's *Journal.*	
1843			Birth of Henry James.
1848	Emancipation of slaves in French West Indian islands.		
1850			Hawthorne's *The Scarlet Letter.*
1851			Melville's *Moby Dick.*
1856		Birth of Sigmund Freud.	
1859	Beginning of importation of Chinese indentured labor to West Indies.		
1861			American Civil War.
1863			Slavery in United States abolished by Lincoln.
1865	Morant Bay riots in Jamaica (followed by Crown Colony reforms).		
1868			Birth of W. E. B. DuBois, Negro sociologist, writer, and militant black activist.
1872			Birth of Paul Laurence Dunbar,

	Caribbean	Europe (esp. Britain)	America
			leading poet of later "Harlem Renaissance."
1885			Birth of Ezra Pound.
1888			Birth of T. S. Eliot.
1889	Birth of Claude McKay (Jamaica).		
1891		Gaugin travels to Tahiti.	
1895		Marconi invents wireless telegraphy.	
1898			Birth of Ernest Hemingway.
1901			First wireless communication between Europe and U.S.
1902		Conrad's *Heart of Darkness*.	
1903	"Tom Redcam's" *Becka's Buckra Baby* (first issue of "All Jamaica Library").		First flight by Wright brothers.
1905– 1914	Emigration of Jamaican workers to Canal Zone.		Panama Canal completed.
1906– 1919			Race riots in United States. Emergence of "Father Divine" sect in black America.
1913	De Lisser's *Jane's Career* (Jamaica).	Einstein's theory of relativity.	
1914– 1918		First World War.	
1917		Russian Bolshevik revolution.	United States enters World War.

	Caribbean	Europe (esp. Britain)	America
1918		Rutherford splits the atom.	
1920– 1929			"Harlem Renaissance." Prohibition in United States.
1923		USSR established.	
1925			Scott Fitzgerald's The Great Gatsby.
1928	McKay's Home to Harlem publ. in United States.	D. H. Lawrence's Lady Chatterly's Lover.	
1929			Wall Street crash. Beginning of world depression.
1930		Death of D. H. Lawrence.	
1929– 1930	Trinidad (two issues), ed. by Alfred Mendes.		
1931– 1933	The Beacon (twenty-eight issues), ed. by Albert Gomes.		
1933	McKay's Banana Bottom.		
1934	Alfred Mendes's Pitch Lake.		
1936	C. L. R. James's Minty Alley.		

CHAPTER 1

Pioneers

I *H. G. De Lisser (1878–1944):*
Jane's Career *(1914)*

THE plot of the novel is simple, conventional, and linear, as one
would expect in a novel written for serialization in a newspaper.[1]
Jane Burrell, a young and innocent village girl, goes to the busy capital city, Kingston, to become an apprentice domestic servant in the
lower-middle-class home of the mulatto Mrs. Mason. In spite of her
resilience and natural good humor, she is unable to cope with Mrs.
Mason's subtle victimizing and runs away to share a room in a slum
"yard" with a good-hearted virago, Sathyra. Victimized again, thanks
to her own good looks and Sathyra's jealousy, she leaves, after a quarrel, and lives by herself. Pursued by her lascivious employer, Jane
finally attracts the attentions of a desirable colored underforeman,
Vincent Broglie. He extricates Jane from an impending and unwelcome affair with her employer by having the good sense to accept
her proposal of marriage. The novel ends with a happily married Jane
living in a respectable part of Kingston, "perfectly contented at last,
and dreaming of no higher fortune" (p. 295). Summarized like this,
the novel might appear to be of only limited interest; but *Jane's Career* is essentially about emancipation; and Jane's rise from the poverty and servitude of her role as a domestic can be seen as an emancipation from a form of slavery. Her escape, first from the proverty and
restrictions of rural family life and then from a disadvantaged role in
society, represents the emancipation of the individual spirit.

The novel opens with Jane, poised for her journey to Kingston, being catechized by the village elder, Daddy Buckram:

"Jane," he continued impressively after a pause, "Kingston is a very big
an' wicked city, an' a young girl like you, who de Lord has blessed wid a
good figure an' a face, must be careful not to keep bad company. Satan

23

goeth about like a roaming lion in Kingston. . . . Don't stay out in de street in de night. . . . If sinners entice thee, consent thou not. Now, tell me what I say to you." (p. 3)

The later reference to Daddy Buckram's "semi-spiritual labours" and his portrayal as a pompous, self-conscious character is not merely an attempt to produce a comic stereotype. Kenneth Ramchand, in *The West Indian Novel and Its Background*, sees De Lisser's treatment of Daddy Buckram as an example of the white author's indulgent, superior attitude to his black characters. This is true to a certain extent, but the fact is that the young people are no longer content with village life and Jane and her friends all long to go to the big city. The urban drift has begun and rural society is changing. Daddy Buckram is already something of an anachronism. Jane is asked by her friends about Daddy Buckram's advice:

"Him say I musn't have nothing to do wid de Kingston bouys, for dem is all a roarin' lion," answered Jane.
"Dat is all foolishness," said the eldest decisively. "Some is good an' some is bad." (p. 6)

De Lisser does not, like most of his contemporaries, romanticize peasant life, nor does he (as Thomas H. MacDermot [under pseud. Tom Redcam] does in *One Brown Girl and—; A Jamaican Story*. Kingston, 1909) sentimentalize his black heroine. Jane is attractive, but she is hardy and realistic. After a description of the beautiful Jamaican landscape through which Jane walks on her way to Kingston, one reads:

Such scenes were familiar to Jane, and roused her admiration not at all. She hardly glanced to right or left as she trudged on; never once did she reflect that she was leaving all this. . . . (p. 35)

In Kingston, dazzled by the vigorous life of the city, Jane meets the Mason family, for whom De Lisser reserves an obvious contempt. Mrs. Mason's mulatto pretensions to middle-class respectability are shown to involve little more than a bourgeois clutter of polished furniture and a series of petty squabbles between mistress and servant. The Mason children are uniformly unlovely. De Lisser seems to be criticizing the Masons not because they are householders aspiring, by virtue of their light brown skins, toward the social eminence of the white Creoles like De Lisser himself, but because their role is one of *imperfect*, vulgar mimicry. Mrs. Mason is humiliated by the servant, Sarah, who demands severance pay when fired and is threatened with police action by Mrs. Mason. She is forced, however, to pay her when the black policeman arrives and is sympathetic to Sarah. But in a later conflict with another servant, Amanda, Mrs. Mason triumphs, ironically, because of *Amanda's* social pretensions as a self-consciously married woman and churchgoer. " 'The church is making ladies and gentlemen of everybody' " (p. 120), Mrs. Mason observes, and proceeds to trap Amanda into a precipitate resignation. Two pretentious types clash and Mrs. Mason, the wilier, wins. Cecil, Mrs. Mason's devious nephew, is used by De Lisser to point up Jane's blend of naturalness and sagacity. She keeps his first gift, a three-penny piece, but feels it necessary to give in to his slimy attentions. Jane learns quickly, however, and soon (as Cecil discovers) becomes a wiser, more positive individual. His second gift (a shilling, his acknowledgment of her growing worth) does not interfere with her plan to escape from the household. Jane feels she has earned her shilling: Mrs. Mason's careful counting of the household cutlery reveals that she has stolen nothing.

Her career now reaches its second stage. Her "slavery" has been "abolished" and her roommate, Sathyra, gets her a job on the assembly line of a liquor-bottling factory. She is now a member of an urban group, a labor force with some power. The pay is better, conditions are reasonable, and she has achieved a higher social status. She is now "Miss Burrell" among her fellow-workers, who are also women. De Lisser's descriptions of the humble but enjoyable "bread-kind" and salt-fish meal which Sathyra prepares with Jane's help, their visit to a local dance, the novelty and excitement of Kingston at night, show an observant and sympathetic eye, in spite of his frequently obtrusive, authorial presence. Sathyra's independence of spirit is celebrated without condescension or sentimentality; and when the inevitable quarrel arises and she makes it clear that Jane is unwelcome because she has become a potential rival, Jane, now more experienced in human relationships, takes the initiative. She moves out and "for the first time in her life she was thrown absolutely on her own resources" (p. 200).

The third stage of her emancipation has now been reached. She is free as an individual, has her own room, and is her own mistress. But the corollary of this new freedom is her growing sense of loneliness and isolation. Independence brings its own problems. The new foreman, Mr. Curden, fortyish, married, and respectable, becomes a nuisance, then a threat. Jane finds that to be a single woman, an independent individual in a coercive, patriarchal society, is a complex and worrying situation. She has to use all her experience and wit to keep Mr. Curden at arm's length without endangering her job. It is a measure of De Lisser's fairness and artistic control that he makes Mr. Curden's infatuation with Jane and his growing exasperation with her delaying tactics seem reasonable enough to gain a measure of our sympathy:

"You simply playin' with me, that's what it is!" snapped Mr. Curden. "If y'u don't want to say yes, say the other thing; there is as good fish in the sea as ever came out of it, and I am not going to kill meself because of you. But I don't mean you to make a fool of me any longer." (pp. 252–53)

Vincent Broglie, the brown, marriageable printer's underforeman, has already entered Jane's life, however, so help is at hand. But there is no sudden romantic alliance between Vincent and Jane. He is well off by Jane's standards, not in the least pretentious, and eminently suitable as a husband, but he is more concerned with his role as spokesman for the Printer's Union strikers and with his political future. Jane's attractiveness is noted, but produces no emotional upheaval in his fairly self-regarding life. De Lisser again avoids the trap of romantic cliché by allowing Jane to prick the balloon of Vincent's incipient egotism. She attends the strikers' meeting and observes the proceedings with a practical though not fully comprehending eye. To her the proposed strike seems misdirected:

". . . If you leave your good job wid a lot of other people, none of them can help you; an' suppose any one go behind your back an' ask for it, what you would do?" This aspect of the matter Vincent did not care to dwell upon, especially as the possibility of it had occurred to himself more than once. (p. 261)

De Lisser is here clearly using Jane's practical, pragmatic peasant wisdom (". . . You know how Jamaica people stand . . .") to reinforce an authorial disapproval of the half-educated militancy of the strikers; but Jane is drawing upon her own very real experience of the problems of independence. She has accepted Mr. Curden's barbed offer of a rent-free apartment, having reluctantly been forced to place survival before ideals. " 'Can't do better,' " she says, a little defiantly, to Vincent, " 'an' it's no use forming independent when y'u know that y'u can't afford it' " (p. 282). She impulsively confesses her feelings for him: " 'I wish it was you, Mr. Vin!' " (p. 283), and then, emboldened by the thought of a life as Mr. Curden's mistress, she proposes. Vincent, whose basic decency and good sense were never in doubt, quickly recognizes the value of Jane's love.

The novel ends with the white wedding which is the prelude to their new life in the respectable, middle-class society of Campbell's Town:

In her white muslin dress, with her hair done up with ribbons, wearing high-heeled shoes and looking as though she had been born to entertaining guests, Jane is not very like the little girl we saw sitting mute and frightened as she drove into Kingston with Mrs. Mason. She is not much like the girl we saw sharing apartments with Sathyra. . . . It is Jane perfectly contented at last, and dreaming of no higher fortune. It is Jane, who now herself employs a schoolgirl, who submissively calls her Miss Jane, and obeys her slightest command. (p. 295)

De Lisser seems, at the end of the novel, to have lost sympathy for (or lost interest in) his heroine. The tone has here become somewhat patronizing and one feels that "such a detached attitude at the end does not accord with the involvement in the longer central sections of the novel" (Ramchand in *The West Indian Novel and Its Background*, p. 58). But this does not mean that De Lisser's approach has been ironic, or that the last chapter of the book shows merely a failure of sympathy for his black heroine. Rather, it is a failure of imagination, and (under the circumstances) perhaps excusable. De Lisser's knowledge of the rural or proletariat life of Jamaica was, inevitably, limited and circumscribed by his social and political convictions. The fact that he was a white Creole, and therefore identified quite readily with a European world-view, makes his insights into Jane's world the more remarkable. That he could visualize "no higher fortune" for her than a "white wedding" and middle-class respectability is hardly surprising. What *is* clear, and perhaps more to the point, is that Jane, as a married woman and householder, has earned her advance in social status: it is a genuine emancipation, achieved with dignity and intelligence, and (in contrast to the Mrs. Masons of her world) will help to provide, one feels, the nucleus of an authentic black urban middle class. It is perhaps ironic that De Lisser, resisting the idea of self-government for Jamaica and resenting the rise of the colored bour-

geoisie, died in May 1944, only six months before adult suffrage and
self-rule were made possible by the granting of a new constitution for
Jamaica.

Jane's Career, then, despite De Lisser's last-minute failure—a failure of imaginative vision as much as of sympathy or interest—is an
important first novel. It may be seen as analogous to the emancipation of the black West Indian in a white and mulatto-ordered society.
Jane's progress from poor peasant to member of an urban work force
to middle-class respectability via a white wedding does not necessarily illustrate an amused, authorial irony. In the West Indies, early attempts at cultural indigenization were heavily tainted by an obdurate
respect for the values of a white, "pedigree" society. Jane's triumph is
a personal and very substantial one in a society still unaware of its
true identity and then, as now, reluctant to acknowledge the individual worth and status of its women. Jane's Career is the first West Indian novel of substance, the first to have a black central character, the
first appearance of a full-fledged fictional heroine.

But Jane's success, her rise from the poverty and restrictions of
rural life and urban slum, remains only a private achievement, un-
characteristic of the social class she represents. Roger Mais (1905–
1955), writing nearly forty years after the publication of Jane's Career, attempted, in The Hills Were Joyful Together (1953), to expose
the continuing social injustice that lay behind the squalor and frustration of the urban black Jamaican yard-dwellers. That "community of
feeling" among the poor which, in Jane's Career, is simply a part of
life, becomes in Mais's book a miracle of survival. The "New Day"
heralded by the constitutional changes in 1944 had been only a beginning, and independence (as Jane had found) brought in its train even
more urgent problems of identity and individual integrity.

II   C. L. R. James (b. 1901):
Minty Alley (1936)

The most active and gifted member of the Beacon group, James
said that he wrote Minty Alley "purely to amuse myself one sum-
mer." [2] For some time he had been interested in the literary possibilities of "yard" life, and had published a short story, "Triumph," [3]
which dealt with the picturesque life in a Port-of-Spain "barrack-
yard." James had actually decided to live in such a yard in order to

experience the life of its inhabitants at first hand: "I went to live there, the people fascinated me, and I wrote about them from the point of view of an educated youthful member of the black middle class." [4] In *Minty Alley*, James drew on this experience to illustrate not only what he saw as the natural *joie de vivre* of the slumdwellers, their ability to transcend repressive surroundings, but also the possibilities for mutual enrichment which might come from a middle-class involvement with, and understanding of, the "yard" folk. Mr. Haynes, a young, middle-class Negro orphaned by the death of his mother, decides to look for cheap lodgings in a slum yard to escape both loneliness and the expense of living in his parents' large, mortgaged home. His faithful servant, Ella, tries to dissuade him, but he persists, and takes a room in No. 2 Minty Alley, where he becomes involved in the life of the yard community. The others respect his higher social status as an educated man, a householder, and a white-collar worker and he uses his position as "father-confessor" and ombudsman to the residents to keep the unstable yard relationships from becoming too explosive. He enjoys this new life, gaining a measure of maturity during the process (thanks partly to an affair with young Maisie, the fiery-tempered beauty of the yard), and is very unhappy when, owing to the death of Benoit, one of the yard's most vital characters, and the insoluble conflict between Maisie and her aunt, Mrs. Rouse, the bereaved landlady of the yard, the community disbands and the property is sold. Haynes goes back to his dull, middle-class life, which had been temporarily heightened by the experience of No. 2 Minty Alley, which itself, inevitably, undergoes change, becoming a respectable, residential area.

As this summary of the plot suggests, *Minty Alley*, like *Jane's Career*, is intended by its author to be a sympathetic study of slum life from a middle-class viewpoint. Where the white De Lisser distances his black characters by a detached, objectively observing eye, however, James's stance is one of subjective involvement. He attempts this through his black character, Mr. Haynes, who functions as an extension of his author's voice and sympathies. From the outset James is clearly an advocate for lower-class vitality as opposed to the dullness and snobbery of middle-class life. When Haynes, worried about the future, summons the fat, black, and faithful servant, Ella, she comes instantly, her face shining "with perspiration and good nature" (p. 19), and refuses to accept an invitation to sit down. Haynes reflects upon the pernicious effect of the class system which has bred the "perfect" servant and the "perfect" mistress.

The influence of his dead mother still dominated the house. She was a perfect mistress, but never would she have asked Ella to sit down. And Ella remained standing. (p. 19)[5]

Haynes, at twenty, is not, however, happy with his middle-class existence even though he knows no other, and was being groomed for higher education in England and a profession in medicine before the untimely death of his mother, whose plans for his future "ever since he had known himself, he had known and accepted" (p. 22). One suspects that James is setting Haynes up as an authorial voice, rather than as a character in his own right. The suspicion grows when we find that Haynes's emotional background is almost a *tabula rasa*. An only child who has had no friends ("no friends—no, not one," p. 22) and no relations "that mattered," who "shrank from his mother's middle-aged friends" and continues living in the house (after her death) "from sheer inertia," Haynes is ripe for Life. Indeed, James himself seems to feel that his protagonist is rather too obviously being prepared for the imprint of Experience (to be provided by Minty Alley), so he takes another tack:

His life was empty. He did not think these things out clearly, but he knew them as people are aware of things without putting them into words. The sea of life was beating at the walls which enclosed him. (p. 23)

Having rather hurriedly prepared us for Haynes's extraordinary decision to become a slum tenant (and, in the West Indies of the 1930s, such a decision would have been considered eccentric indeed), James virtually pushes Haynes into the teeming life of Minty Alley:

"Where did you say that room was, Ella?"
"Two streets from here, sir, No. 2, Minty Alley. . . ."
"Well, we'll go there."
"But you haven't seen the place, sir. I don't think you'll like it. There are a lot of people there, sir. Ordinary people."
"So much the better. I am sure I will like it. 2, Minty Alley. It sounds good. . . ." (p. 24)

Later on we are told that "Haynes knew that he would take it, had, indeed, decided to do so from the time Ella had mentioned the place" (p. 26). As it turns out, Mr. Haynes (he is referred to only as "Mr. Haynes" or "Haynes") is little more than a narrative device used by

James to illustrate the essentially worthwhile and vibrant life of the slum community. The life of the yard is not romanticized, but the squalid condition and behavior of its inhabitants are carefully offset against their innate dignity and goodness of heart. The appearance of Mrs. Rouse, the landlady, seen through Haynes's eyes, conveys perfectly this mixture of outer censure and inner approval:

She had no need to apologise for her appearance. She was a woman somewhere in the forties, fat, yet with a firmness and shapeliness of figure which prevented her from looking gross. Her face was a smooth lightbrown with a fine acquiline nose and well-cut firm lips. The strain of white ancestry responsible for the nose was not recent, for her hair was coarse and essentially negroid. Her apron was dirty, but the dress below was clean. . . . She made a slight bow and turned and led the way, carrying herself erect with a mature grace and dignity which Haynes thought assumed for the occasion but which he learnt to know later were natural to her. (p. 26)

The blend of qualities is significant. Mrs. Rouse's light brown skin and aquiline features seem to *mitigate* the "coarse," negroid hair just as her stately bearing contradicts her humble status, and the clean dress compensates for the dirty apron. In fact this balance of physical characteristics is consonant with the woman's role in the novel, for it is Mrs. Rouse who emerges as an all-suffering, hard-working matriarch faithful to her sense of Christian duty and to her irresistible but errant lover, Benoit. Haynes's confidence in her as landlady is the correlative of his faith in the authenticity of life in Minty Alley.

Haynes himself is given a middle-class pomposity that seems extravagant, in the circumstances. He moves in to No. 2 with his personal servant, Ella, graciously declining Mrs. Rouse's offer of full board:

"Thank you very much, Mrs. Rouse. But Ella, my servant, is in charge of everything. She washes the clothes, cooks my meals and so on. I could not think of carrying on without Ella, she has been with me so long and understands me so well." (p. 27)

and Mrs. Rouse is overcome with surprise and gratitude when he "quite spontaneously" shakes her hand. In attempting to establish Haynes's superior status, James overbalances into near parody, and his character tends, as a result, to remain one-dimensional. His is the novel's observing eye, nevertheless, and in this role Haynes is kept

fully occupied. He meets Benoit, the womanizer who has, for eigh-
teen years, been Mrs. Rouse's paramour:

He was a rather big man with a slight paunch. His very black face was
undistinguished-looking, neither handsome nor ugly. The very dark skin
and curly hair showed traces of Indian blood. The only thing one might
have noticed was a rather cruel mouth below the sparse moustache.
(p. 30)

Benoit is the highly sexed, irresponsible type: the immoderate element of yard life which will eventually destroy the cohesion of Minty
Alley society and hasten his own death. And sure enough, it is this
exciting element of suppressed, hidden sexual energy that convinces
Haynes, just as he begins to feel that he has made a mistake, that life
in Minty Alley will yield a rewarding experience. He discovers a
crack in the wall of his room, and, peeping through, sees Benoit kiss-
ing Wilhelmina, the servant-girl, with fierce passion. Haynes is not
merely surprised; he is overcome with delirious joy. Here, indeed, is
Life in the Raw:

He was suddenly no longer sleepy. . . . He balanced himself on the small
of his back and kicked his feet up in the air. To read of these things was
one thing, to hear and see them was another. . . . And here now he had
been pitch-forked into the heart of the eternal triangle. (p. 37)

Elated, Haynes eagerly prepares to observe the general activities of
his neighbors with a certain deliberateness, like a man at the theater:

. . . He opened his door and sat waiting to see the household set about
its daily tasks. The stage, he felt, was set for a terrific human drama.
(p. 38)

And this is precisely what is wrong with James's use of Haynes as
observer. Given his cloistered, middle-class upbringing, Haynes
would conceivably enjoy the role of voyeur in such a sexually liberal
society. But as a disinterested observer of the whole community "setting about its daily tasks" he is hardly credible; especially when
James has him enlarge and camouflage his peephole "so as to command a wide and comprehensive view of the whole yard" (p. 54).
This transparent device is soon dropped, however, and Haynes becomes instead the willing recipient of all the gossip and news of the

yard. Everyone unburdens to him, and in this way his role of observer
is maintained with less authorial subterfuge. It is true that Haynes is
presented as a naif outsider, understandably fascinated by a way of
life outside of his experience; but the middle-class dismay which he
feels when the possibility of a scandal arises is, one feels, too easily
discounted and nullified by his curiosity about the affairs of Minty
Alley. One night Mrs. Rouse goes for Benoit with a kitchen knife, and,
genuinely alarmed, Mr. Haynes thinks of taking Ella's advice to
leave. He doesn't, because "he felt that to leave the house would be
an unbearable wrench" (p. 77). This is hard to credit since, at this
point, Haynes has little real connection with the people of the yard,
and still feels that Ella's advice is sound: "if anything did happen," he
thinks, "there would be a teriffic scandal. And he might lose his job"
(p. 77). James's answer is to remove Ella from the scene (she falls ill
and is sent off to her mother in the country), thereby leaving Haynes
free to become more intimately involved in the activities of the yard's
inhabitants.

Maisie, Mrs. Rouse's nubile, brown-skinned niece, takes over Ella's
role and is "constantly and in official charge of him" (p. 94). This is
the beginning of Haynes's new maturity, but even here there is a deliberateness about it that borders on cliché:

He realised that whatever he said would carry weight with them, and
with this realisation came a sense of responsibility and increasing confidence. . . . How these women centred around a man. "It's good to be a
man," said Haynes to himself, and girded himself for the task of showing
both Maisie and himself what a man he was. (p. 154)

Maisie is a very easy lay, however, and Haynes "to his astonishment
did what he liked with her" (p. 168). To be fair, James avoids any hint
of Romantic Love in the affair, being concerned rather to show sex as
a natural physical activity among the lower classes and to use
Haynes's new intimacy with Maisie to furnish further details of Minty
Alley life. Benoit leaves Mrs. Rouse for the "other woman," the fair-
skinned Nurse Jackson, and Maisie (who has encouraged their liaison
for purposes of petty blackmail) becomes a fierce antagonist to Mrs.
Rouse. Haynes finds himself caught in the crossfire and finally takes
Maisie's part. But news comes of Benoit, deserted in turn by the
nurse, dying in the hospital, and Mrs. Rouse, unable to see him that
night, learns the following day of his death. Maisie manages to secure
a passage on a ship bound for America, and Minty Alley society drifts

apart after Mrs. Rouse, a broken woman, sells the property. The faithful Ella is sent for and promptly takes charge of Haynes, who moves into a more respectable neighborhood. He has had his experience of yard life, but the experiment, one feels, will not be repeated.

Minty Alley, as Kenneth Ramchand writes in his introduction to the 1971 edition of the book, is concerned to show "the mutually impoverishing alienation of the educated West Indian from the people" (p. 13). James's partisan approach, however, his determination to present the yard community as essentially a healthy one in terms of its "fullness of life," precludes the possibility of any real exploration of the gap between the writer and the people he writes about. The book is rather an indictment of the pallid middle-class who uphold status at the expense of genuine living. And it is a measure of James's failure to explore the possibilities of mutual enrichment between the classes that Haynes is shown as having gained only a rather superficial confidence as a result of his experience. He is no longer shy about sexual intercourse and is more self-assertive with his employer. What the yard community gain from his residence there is even less substantial, and perhaps a trifle ironic: they find confirmation in Haynes of their image of what the educated middle-class gentleman should be. The whole yard learns to respect and seek his opinion, and Maisie's regard for his kindness to her expresses itself as "an unwearied personal attendance on him week in week out" (p. 211). It is a devotion to Haynes reminiscent of Ella's. When the Minty Alley group breaks up, Mrs. Rouse is concerned about her model boarder:

> "You must send for Ella, Mr. Haynes."
> "Yes, I know."
> "She will come?"
> "Wherever she is working she will come if I go for her," said Haynes. Ella came at the first call, got rooms for him and he moved into them on the first of October. . . . (p. 243)

This is not to deny the novel's occasional insights into the "yard" ethos. The ritual beating of the wretched Sonny by his mother, Nurse Jackson, is shown to be an expression of concern and ownership that is both playful and sadistic. When the hapless boy, taking refuge in Mr. Haynes's room, is encouraged to go back to his as yet unappeased mother, she says, with grim humor:

> ". . . It's no use your bringing him. He has to come to me by himself. And he knows it. . . . Doggie! Doggie! Look bone," she said. (p. 45)

James conveys the complex motives for the brutal beating—a familiar enough phenomenon in West Indian slum life—by showing Mrs. Jackson (a near-white, middle-class woman fallen on evil days) to be an intelligent and efficient nurse, but a rejected wife carrying a destructive sexual grievance against all men. Her subsequent enslavement and rejection of Benoit underscores this complexity of character and (ironically) illustrates the pernicious effect of her superior but warped intelligence on the simpler folk of the yard. The nurse's "refined qualities" and professionalism—traditionally middle-class virtues—add nothing to, but rather disrupt, the yard community.

Whatever its shortcomings, *Minty Alley* is an interesting and important novel of the "yard," if only because of its author's "inwardness" with the Trinidadian "low-life" dialect and character, and his obvious commitment to, and concern for, the despised Folk.

III Roger Mais (1905–1955)

Roger Mais's commitment in *The Hills Were Joyful Together* (1953) is similar to C. L. R. James's, but powered by a vigorously protesting social conscience. The book had been written, he said, "to give the world a true picture of the real Jamaica and the dreadful conditions of the working classes." [6] Mais is here the spokesman for the disadvantaged black community, the "Folk," rather than for the private individual. In *The Hills Were Joyful Together* the "yard" is shown to be a little world in itself where anger, crime, frustration, poverty, and death seem to be the common inheritance, thanks to society's indifference and a vicious penal system. The singing and dancing at the "fish-fry," when the inhabitants of the yard rise, however temporarily, above their constricted existence, is presented as an example of the indomitable spirit which can survive within a "community of feeling." Surjue, the group's most articulate member, is shot escaping from prison and his woman, Rema, dies in a fire which she has started while mentally disturbed. Given the oppression and squalor which make a prison of the lives of these inhabitants, Mais seems to be saying, it is a miracle that such "yard" communities can still survive and contain and share life. Escape from the "yard," however, is denied Mais's characters, for society ostracizes and punishes the free spirit. Mais himself was aware of the middle-class disapproval his work received, and in 1952 he decided to leave Jamaica.

But even in Mais's small oeuvre of three published novels one can discern another, more urgent reason for his self-exile. This is the

growing gulf within the writer himself: a split between two competing demands, one social and communal, the other private and artistic.
It is as if the writer, compelled by the growing urgency of his artistic
vision and the aesthetic demands of his art, turns away from the
"community novel" toward a more private vision. His second published novel, *Brother Man* (1954), is also presented as a "community
drama," more formally structured than *The Hills Were Joyful Together*, and carefully orchestrated to suggest a "community of feeling" caught up, as Mais puts it, "between the covers of the same book
of living" (p. 8). Where, in *Hills*, there is the occasional use of poetic
and symbolic commentary to suggest an atmosphere of foreboding:

The dark shadows beyond our ken crowd in upon us . . . they wait in
silence and drink up in darkness . . . the sun rolls down the sky without
stay, without sound. . . . (p. 150)[7]

in *Brother Man* there is an explicit choric device—the "Chorus of
People in the Lane"—which introduces each of the five chapters.
The novel's scene is set and the life of the community suggested by
the first "chorus":

The tongues of the lane clack-clack almost continuously, going up and
down the full scale of human emotions. . . . They clack on street corners, where the ice-shop hangs out a triangular red flag. . . . Around the
yam-seller's barrow . . . where the neighbours meet in the Chinese gro-
cery shop on the corner. . . . (p. 7)

As the novel proceeds, these "choruses" become more and more like
stage directions, however, and in the final chapter, just before
Brother Man, the novel's hero, is rejected and beaten by his own people, one reads in the "chorus":

There is a feeling of excitement in the air. It is reflected in the attitudes
of the people. They are more alert-looking, their faces less habitually
tired-seeming, care-worn. . . . The moon is late in coming up; there is no
moon tonight. (p. 138)

Brother Man is self-appointed spokesman for Rastafarianism,[8] then
in its infancy, and he represents (as his real name, John Power, suggests) the native, God-fearing element of religious "grounding"
which allows him to act as faith-healer and confessor to the poor and

downtrodden of the community. In fact, the novel is essentially a recounting of the career of Brother Man, whose genuine goodness is not
finally understood by the very folk with whom he is so deeply concerned. Cast in the role of a Christ figure, a man of sorrows ac-
quainted with grief, Bra' Man (as he is called) is also the good counterpart of the community's obeah healer, the charlatan Bra' Ambo.
Unlike his unscrupulous rival, Bra' Man (after a vision in which he is
advised to "go, and anoint yourself, and fast for three days") has a
genuine power of healing, which he uses compassionately and not for
profit. But the public are misled by the fake Rastafarians in their
midst. After a report of the murder of a young couple by an unkempt
and bearded black assailant, a group of people incensed against all
bearded, Rasta-like men attacks and beats the innocent Bra' Man in
the street. Bra' Man's followers have almost all deserted him by now,
and, like Christ, he is scourged and left to die. A faithful follower,
Nathaniel, and two women take him home and look after him, however. The style of the novel is here decidedly biblical: "They washed
his wounds between them, and dressed them and bound them up, and
laid him in his bed. And when they had made an end of all these
things, Nathaniel went to his own home. But the two women
. . . kept watch through the night." "On the evening of the third
day" (p. 190) he recovers, and the novel ends with Minette (the young
country girl, drifting into prostitution, whom he has "reclaimed" and
is now his closest disciple) standing at his side by the window, looking
up "above the rooftops where that great light glowed across the sky"
(p. 191). Bra' Man's "vision of certitude," however, seems only the
vaguest hint of a possible change for the better in the community: it is
clear that, as a central, linking figure whose religious presence might
have welded the community of the poor into a whole, Brother Man
has failed. As a spokesman for the Folk he is finally too introspective
and isolated. Indeed, he is something of an enigma. His commitment
to the community is at odds with his private vision of "peace and
love," the Rastafarian credo which provides him with an inner seren-
ity but leaves him detached and passive in the eyes of others. It is
what one critic[9] has called Brother Man's "individuation" from "the
social mutter": the drift away from the collective sound toward the
alienated, private voice.

This is quite clearly the dilemma of Jake, the hero of Mais's last
published novel, *Black Lightning* (1955). Jake, the blacksmith of a
tiny, rural village by day and a sculptor by night, is both a society-
oriented artisan as well as a private artist. He stubbornly refuses the

advice of the village elders, who feel that, as an educated man, he ought to look for a more suitable job. Jake's reply is admirably right-minded:

I might have found other things to do that I liked better, that would bring in more money, perhaps; but nothing would have served the needs of a greater number of people. My father owned this shop before me. He didn't think himself too good to be a blacksmith. (p. 101)

His commitment to a social role, however, leaves only the night-time for his wood-carving, an artistic urge that he clearly cannot ignore, and about which he feels some anxiety. Jake, working on his Samson figure by the light of a lamp held by young Miriam, has a sudden sense of panic:

The most important thing left to him in life now was his carving, and something was happening to that. He could feel it slipping away from him in some intangible manner. . . . His hand trembled, faltered, stopped. . . . (pp. 82–83)

But the moment passes, and he is able to resume the work:

. . . His vision cleared. He had been at it too closely for too long, that was all. His vision cleared. He saw . . . the coming into being of some-thing, the image of which was locked within his mind. (p. 83)

Indeed, Jake's nocturnal carving has an obsessional note, for he identifies with the Samson-figure, seeing himself as a strong man threatened by weakness, the need to depend on others. The community-minded Jake is really a lonely and proud individual at heart, and his jealously guarded carving represents this private, artis-tic self. As the work proceeds, Jake comes to be more and more de-pendent on others. His wife, Estella, deserts him (a "betrayal," one feels, that is intended to remind us of Delilah's treatment of Samson), and his friendship with the accordian-playing hunchback, Amos, be-comes more complex:

He felt uncomfortable, thinking about himself and Amos. . . . He thought, if I was weak and helpless like Amos, I would need somebody strong to lean upon. And the thought filled him with resentment. . . . He resented, with a strong, whole man's resentment, any thought of being dependent upon anyone for anything. (p. 69)

Earlier, we had been told that Jake "couldn't bear to be crossed" (p. 37) and Estella leaves him because his self-sufficiency is in fact a form of egoism. Steve, Estella's lover, puts it bluntly during an argument with her: "You know he doesn't love you, really. It's himself he loves. He's just wrapped up in *that!*" (p. 31). Jake is certainly a monolithic hero. From the outset of the book, where the characters are introduced to us as they enter the pastoral wood, Jake is the center of each discussion. First Miriam and Glen, the young lovers quarreling and making up, then Amos, alone, to be found later by Bess, the housekeeper, looking for Miriam. Estella, Jake's wife, and her lover, Steve, enter the wood next and finally "Jake, too, came a-walk into the wood" (p. 33). The wood itself functions (in a symbolic way, reminiscent of D. H. Lawrence's *Lady Chatterly's Lover*) as the repository of a natural life force which transcends the characters' petty squabbles and, eventually, death itself. At the end of the book, Glen and Miriam meet, reconciled at last, in the wood:

And the tall trees stood still again, as though they had never moved at all; as though they were possessed of a secret that awed them to silence. (pp. 221–22)

In a hushed voice Miriam says: "If I had to die, I think I would like to die out here" (p. 221). As the lovers stand close together, listening to the sound of the birds, a shot rings out in another part of the wood. Jake, blinded by lightning, disillusioned with his art, has committed suicide.

This is never explicitly stated, but the reader has seen Jake's gradual drift toward death. Earlier in the novel, his carving had been roundly denounced by Old Mother Coby, the village Cassandra:

"The Lord said thou shalt not make any graven images; and that's what you been doing up there," pointing to the loft with her stick. Her thin voice quavered on: "with all the mystery and goings-on about it. God is not mocked. Repent! . . ." (p. 76)

Jake's carving represents a Promethean *hubris* which creates within him a sense of secret guilt. Jake knows that it was not merely Samson's betrayal by Delilah that brought humiliation, blindness, and death, "but what must have lain secretly underneath . . . that the Bible never gave any clue of at all" (p. 60). In the climactic scene in the book when, during a thunderstorm, he takes an apprehensive

Amos to see the carving in the loft, the link between the Samson-figure and Jake is clear. The figure has become that of the *blind* Samson, leaning on the shoulder of a boy. Worse, it has begun to resemble Jake. Amos, horrified at this development, confirms Jake's anxious, insistent questioning:

"I see it, Jake. What—what you wanted me to see. . . . It ain't Samson anymore, is what you mean; ain't it?" (p. 112)

As Amos scrambles down from the loft, the lightning strikes and Jake falls unconscious. Like Milton's tragic hero in *Samson Agonistes*, Jake, convinced that he has been blinded for his sin of pride, broods inwardly. Estella returns to the village, but it is too late. Jake destroys his carving and, finally, himself. Unable to reconcile the demands of social awareness—his blacksmith's job[10]—with the more urgent demands of his art, he chooses self-destruction as a means of escape from an insoluble crisis of loyalties.

Mais, like his character Jake, began his career with a sense of social duty; the need to champion the cause of the despised and neglected black urban poor. As the development of his work suggests, however, the split between his role as spokesman for a community and his concern as an individual artist continued to grow. It was, as E. K. Brathwaite recognizes, "a radical West Indian problem. Can we [writers] stay with the tropical drought, or do we emigrate?" [11] Mais's decision to leave Jamaica in 1952 was the (perhaps) inevitable result of an imaginative talent outgrowing its native soil; but Mais nevertheless felt it as "exile." In 1952, in his article "Why I Love and Leave Jamaica," [12] he spoke of his society's "lack of values" and its "want of personal integrity." The Philistines had won. Roger Mais returned to Jamaica two years later, already fatally ill with cancer. His funeral service was held in Kingston's Coke Church, the same church in which De Lisser's Jane achieves her "apotheosis" via a white wedding. It is a nice irony, illustrating the gulf between the superficial "solution" of *Jane's Career* and the harsh reality of Mais's commitment to his role as artist. It also illustrates the changing emphasis in the development of West Indian fiction: with Mais, the theme of cultural and social emancipation is expanded to include the problem of "divided loyalties": the conflict between the claims of society and of art. This conflict, however, has another, most disturbing aspect; and it is in the work of Edgar Mittelholzer, Mais's contempo-

rary, that the problem of "divided loyalties," as a cultural and psychological dilemma, can be seen most clearly.

IV *Edgar Mittelholzer (1909–1965)*

Born in British Guiana, a swarthy first child of European-looking
parents, Mittelholzer was a great disappointment to his father, "a
confirmed negrophobe" [13] whose resentment instilled in the child a
sense of having been wronged by nature. His work reflects a serious
conflict of loyalties, a consistent and conscious wish to identify with
the European side of his ancestry while recognizing, at the same
time, his individuality as a West Indian. Mittelholzer apparently believed that strength of will was a prerequisite for happiness, and that
his "Germanic," European blood represented this "strength" while
his "West Indian" blood harbored a "weakness." This attitude undoubtedly led to the psychological disunity which became, in turn,
not only the chief cause of his unhappiness as a man, but also the
main theme of his work as a novelist.

Mittelholzer had intended his first novel, *Corentyne Thunder*
(1941), to be a story about Hindu peasant life on the east coast of
what was then British Guiana. In fact, the most striking theme in the
book is a psychological one: that of "inner division." Geoffry Weldon,
son of a wealthy mulatto plantation owner and a Guyanese Hindu
peasant woman, is torn between loyalty to his father, who wants him
to go abroad to study, and his love for the Corentyne and for Kattree,
the Hindu peasant girl to whom he is related. Geoffry finds it difficult
to choose between these opposing forces, and the dark prophecy he
makes: "One day . . . I'm going to commit suicide, Kattree, and
people will wonder why" (p. 263)[14] is the *crie de coeur* of a man fatally divided within himself. The division between rural and urban,
self and society, gives way in *Corentyne Thunder*, to a more disturbing, though related, *malaise: mulatto angst*. For the first time, the
question of racial admixture as a complicating factor in the "division
of loyalties" becomes a central theme in West Indian fiction.

In *Corentyne Thunder* Mittelholzer is very much the young,
would-be colonial author "writing novels for the people of Britain to
read." [15] After a self-conscious beginning ("A tale we are about to tell
of Ramgolall, the cow-minder") the novel develops as a sympathetic
but unsentimental evocation of Hindu peasant life on the Corentyne,
calculated to interest readers in the United Kingdom who would, of

course, know nothing about this kind of life. The frequent historical and geographical glosses are clearly concessions to the metropolitan reader's ignorance of the book's ethos. Ramgolall, Mittelholzer explains,

> . . . lived on the Corentyne coast of British Guiana, *the only British colony on the mainland of South America.* . . . He was an East Indian *who had arrived in British Guiana in 1898* as an immigrant indentured to a sugar estate. (p. 7, my italics)

Ramgolall has many children, among them Baijan, who "was the owner of a rice-mill in Essequibo, *the largest of the three counties of British Guiana*" (p. 7, my italics). The atmosphere of the flat, wild coast with its swampy savannah lands is conveyed with great accuracy, the result of patient and sensitive observation; and the squalid life of the peasants is repeatedly offset against the stark, sombre beauty of the landscape:

> The grey clouds in the east broke up into filmy fragments that melted overhead, leaving a blue sky streaked faintly with feathery tendrils of cirrus. The savannah glistened wetly in the sunlight, and flocks of white birds settled on its surface, making faint, harsh cries that mingled with the lowing of the calves to form the strange dawn-music that freshened the spirits of Ramgolall. (p. 18)

Mittelholzer adopts a conventional, omniscient attitude to his characters and the style of the writing is occasionally pompous. When Beena suffers an attack of stomach cramp, the result of overwork and undernourishment, the author is not content simply to convey Beena's agony or Ramgolall's sense of alarm and frustration through his characters' own awareness, but enters the narrative in an obtrusive, supervisory manner:

> Beena moaned softly and her breathing came in heavy gusts as though her soul were fatigued with the things of this life. . . . "Talk, na, bettay? Try. You' belly a-hurt?" The moan came again like a portent, like the echo of a horn sounded in the depth of the earth. "The Dark gathers," it seemed to tell the soul of Ramgolall, "and Death cometh with the Dark. Be resigned my son." (pp. 9–10)

The author's intrusion mars an incident which is nevertheless quite convincing:

Ramgolall stood up in a panic, looking all around him. He saw the cows, a group of moving spots, headed for their pen and getting smaller as they went. He could smell their dung mingled with the iodine in the air. (p. 10)

Here, Ramgolall's own consciousness is allowed to function. We are made aware of his helplessness naturally, through his inability to focus his mind on the immediate disaster.

Introducing Geoffry Weldon, Mittelholzer suggests the inner resources of his character by direct authorial comment, but, in so doing, strikes an excessively portentous note:

He had power, a deep, tight-locked power that, one felt, might make a terrible whirl of damage, like a cyclone, if unlocked without warning. Seeing him, one thought of a coppery sky and a dead-smooth sea—the China Sea of Conrad—and a falling barometer. (pp. 52–53)

The author also reveals an occasional weakness for the self-consciously "poetic" phrase, as in his description of the chimneys of the Speyerfield sugar factory as "huge guns of unreckoned age trained upon Eternity" (p. 48), a phrase which is repeated a few paragraphs later. Having chosen to remain omniscient, the author is, as a result, forced to intrude at points in an attempt to explain apparent anomalies in characterization or plot. The sign on the green bus which overtakes Jannee and Beena on the road, for example, presents a problem of this kind to the scrupulous Mittelholzer:

They could see the lettering . . . *Claudette Colbert*, though Beena and Jannee could not tell this from the lettering, not being able to read. They recognised it by its colour and shape, however, and Beena smiled and said: "You' frien' deh inside *Claudette Colbert*." (pp. 48–49)

These infelicities of style and technique are the exception rather than the rule, however, and Mittelholzer's characters, though lacking in depth, nevertheless retain their credibility for the reader. An example of the successful use of the omniscient, authorial technique is in the meeting of Geoffry and Kattree where Geoffry speaks to her about his

own complex emotional problems while her awareness remains outside the range of his remarks, concerned only with external, physical
appearances:

> She never understood him when he spoke to her jumbie. She never tried
> to understand him . . . she would just be silent and listen to the sound of
> his voice until he stopped speaking. (p. 273)

There is also a positive advantage in the use of direct, authorial commentary, for although the author's presence is at times obtrusive, at
least the need to engineer situations, as in C. L. R. James's *Minty
Alley* (where the young middle-class Negro Haynes is at times too
obviously an authorial device used for the objective observation of
working-class life in Trinidad), is happily avoided. Characters' inner
lives in *Corentyne Thunder* are not explored in depth, partly because
Mittelholzer's determined stance as omniscient author/narrator does
not readily permit this kind of development; but also, more importantly, perhaps, because the environment is allowed to loom larger
than the lives of its inhabitants. It is a landscape imbued with an almost living intelligence, but neutral, unknowable, indestructible:

> To the right of them the canal flowed with calm, telling nothing of what
> it knew of the rainstorms and the high winds, and the droughts of years
> gone by, of the stench of dead cows and the thunder of purple clouds.
> Only now and then a *sherriga*[16] would scramble to the surface and claw
> redly at the air, so that two bubbles made a tinkling gurgle and sent rip-
> ples hooping wider and wider into the nothing of the mirrored sky. (p. 57)

In spite of the impression given in the opening lines of the novel,
Ramgolall is not the central figure, and his character is not developed
much beyond his miser's compulsive love of money and his pleasure
at the social and material advancement of his offspring: a trait he
shares with his "local-white" son-in-law, James ("Big Man") Weldon,
whose materialism has a far less understandable basis, and whose aesthetic perspectives are narrower even than Ramgolall's, in spite of his
success as a cattle-rancher, his superior social status, and his well-
furnished, comfortable home. Seated in his chauffeur-driven car,

> Big Man grunted and settled back comfortably against the leather uphol-
> stery, feeling very contented. He looked out at the bright sunshine and

liked it. . . . Gazing out over the flat savannah country, he felt no romantic or poetic thrill. He was merely conscious of a complacent triumph. There lay the land he had conquered. (p. 125)

Life, for him, holds no uncertainties or perplexities:

The whole thing lay before him, complete, void of all mystery. . . . All
that was left for him to do now was to see that the parts continued to
hold together and were not scattered by any disturbing wind. That was
the only real interest life held for him now: the guarding of his property
and his family. (pp. 125–26)

Alongside this monolithic egocentricity, which has its counterpart in
Ramgolall's patient, obsessive hoarding of coins, Mittelholzer places,
without obtrusive moralizing, the enduring, all-encompassing beauty
and menace of the land—what Wilson Harris calls "the open Oudin
savannahs" [17]—a very different world from the well-ordered, domes-
ticated one envisaged by Weldon with such complacency; and one,
we realize as the novel proceeds, which is far more real. Both Ramgolall and Weldon use the land solely to nourish and increase their stock
of cattle, as they have used their wives merely to reproduce their own
seed. The accent is always on the returns on an outlay: nothing is
freely given by either. Weldon sees Sosee, who lives with him as his
mistress, as

. . . a kind of slave—a healthy female slave whom he had brought into
his house to satisfy his sexual needs and to reproduce his kind. . . . He
had taken them from his body as complete seeds and planted them in her
as in fertile soil. . . . (p. 127)

And faced with Kattree's possible pregnancy, Ramgolall's first concern is for his savings and the drain on them which a new life will
create. Sosee's affair with Big Man Weldon had received his sanction
only when it became clear that the alliance would bring lasting material benefits; and Baijan's success in the world, even though it is a
world his father does not understand, brings tears of pride to
Ramgolall's eyes, for the son's marriage is a social and financial triumph which redounds on the father:

Ramgolall groaned and nodded his head, smiling. "Baijan great boy," he
said. . . . "Me na disappoint' in 'e. 'E great boy. 'E bring me honour in

de worl'—like Sosee bring me long time ago. 'E great boy. Me proud to
call 'e me son. Eh-heh." . . . Glancing at him, Kattree saw that his eyes
looked wet in the corners. (p. 208)

Weldon regards his own offspring with a similar, though less forgiv-
able, vulgar pride, the feeling of satisfaction that comes from a sense
of personal power:

Big Man smiled a faint, affectionate smile as he regarded the children. He
always felt oddly content and proud when he saw them all together like
this. Something glowed pleasantly within him. It made him feel important, generous and big . . . as though he were the wielder of solid power,
even more so than his money gave him. (p. 123)

The differences between poor peasant and rich cattle-rancher are
more significant, however, than the similarities. The miserly Ramgolall is, at least, still in harmony with the landscape, and his life is still
related to the simple needs of the body, the natural cycles of the
land:

He opened his eyes and looked around him, and though everything still
lay cloaked in dark, he knew it was dawn. He knew that the east was fair
like the bellies of the cows in the pen. He heard the lowing of the calves,
who, separated from their mothers, hungered for the milk in the swollen
udders. Maw-aw-w-w, went the calves, and Ramgolall felt the blood of
life run afresh within his veins. This was a new day. (p. 17)

And, although he is proud of the material and social success of his son,
Ramgolall instinctively rejects the pretentious, urbanized way of life
of Baijan and the Ramjits, who represent the rising, "creolized,"
Hindu middle class, no longer tied to the land. It is, incidentally, one
of Mittelholzer's achievements that he is able to present with gentle
irony and considerable insight and economy a graphic picture of the
process of "creolization" at work in the Hindu peasant community of
the Corentyne. In the characterization of Baijan he catches exactly
the brash, energetic tone of the man determined to make his way up
the social ladder—an older, less introverted Mr. Biswas:[18]

"I hear Dr. Matthias buy over ol' Mrs. Clyde' house, eh? Good place, you
know. One o' dese days I got to own a house like dat. Big house wid a
tower and plenty bedrooms and servants, an' a piano fo' Liza to play."
(p. 199)

In the Ramjits' big "two-story house wid de red roof" (p. 201), Mr.
Ramjit, with ostentatious generosity, calls:

"Charlie boy, make you'self useful in deh an' bring out some biscuits an'
soft drinks fo' Beena an' Kattree an' de ol' man. Keep deh mout' occupy
till breakfast time!" (p. 204)[19]

while "Miss Elizabeth Irene Ramjit" (p. 203) plays "Backerollee,
from de tales of Hoffman" (p. 204) on the piano for guests who feel
increasingly uncomfortable and intimidated by the opulence of a living room crowded with furniture and thick rugs on the floor, on the
polished surface of which Beena has already left faint, accusing toe-
prints. Made to feel exposed, awkward, out of place (Joseph Ramjit's
furtive staring at Kattree, who wears no underclothes, makes her, for
the first time in her life, sexually self-conscious), Ramgolall, Beena,
and Kattree do not enjoy their visit. Later, at Baijan's Anglican
church-wedding, their naturalness asserts itself in the face of all the
bourgeois clutter of flowered hats, white gloves, iced cake, and cham-
pagne. Baijan

. . . bought vests and silk panties and brassieres for them in Speyerfield,
and hats trimmed with ribbon and pink flowers. He bought for them, too,
high heeled shoes of shining black leather, but Kattree and Beena over-
balanced and nearly fell down when they tried to walk in them so he had
to buy flat heeled shoes instead. . . . Ramgolall, too, kept wriggling and
fidgeting in the light-grey suit which Baijan had had made for him. During the ceremony he took off his collar and tie and stuffed them into his
coat pocket, and the people in the pews behind him gave muffled snig-
gers. He did not mind, however. He preferred to be laughed at than to be
choked to death. (pp. 287–88)

At the reception they understand neither the forced gaiety nor the
pompous, wordy speeches; and when the parson makes "a queer sign
with his hand," intoning "*In nomine patris et filii et spiritus sancti*"
(p. 289), their incomprehension is complete. On the way home, Ramgolall is sick in the car.

By contrast, the curry-feeds to which they invite their neighbors
whenever the rice harvest has been gathered in, when they sing to the
music of drum, serangee, and sitar, are natural, unpretentious occa-
sions for merrymaking and serve as a tacit comment on the newly
acquired, westernized habits of Baijan and the Ramjits. The drift
away from the land has already begun, however, and cannot be re-

versed. When Ramgolall dies of shock and grief after he discovers
that his canister has been rifled, his death is symbolic of the passing of
another, older way of life: for the canister had contained not only his
hoard of coins, but also a whole past existence:

In it lay stored away all the troubles and pleasures that life had brought
him: kicks and angry words from the overseers, his first marriage—riot and
the shooting by the police, Pagwah festivals, the death of his first wife
and that dark day when his eldest son had got killed in a dray-cart accident, his second marriage, Sosee getting of age and Big Man coming to
take her out, and the birth of Kattree and Beena, Baijan and his provision
shop; all those things, and more, lay hidden in the gloom within his faithful canister. (p. 269)

The death of the old man is linked to Jannee's "new" life, for Beena
steals the money to pay the lawyer who saves Jannee from the gal-
lows; but Ramgolall's death is given a wider, almost cosmic significance: it is a part of the cyclic rhythm of nature, and is foreshadowed
earlier in the book:

Were he to die tonight he should die feeling that he had not lived in vain.
He should die feeling that he had added to the good things of the world.
He had seen the flowering and the ripening of his seed and of his seed's
seed. (p. 89)

This circular pattern of life and death, like the indifferent grinding of
the machinery of the sugar factory—

The red sunshine whitened into noon and waned into orange and still it
went on. Rug-a-rug, rug-a-rug, rug-a-rug: a leisured sound, cold and detached, uncaring, like the sky or the savannah or the stars at night.
(p. 291)

—runs throughout the book. Sukra's baby is born; Boorharry is mur-
dered; Jannee's life is saved; Ramgolall dies; Kattree becomes pregnant.

Big Man Weldon, however, is, unlike Ramgolall, almost completely alienated from the land which, for him, is little more than a
pleasant, or occasionally unpleasant, view from the window of his
speeding car. The sounds of the land like the "dawn-music that
freshened the spirits of Ramgolall" (p. 18) are, by Weldon's ears, either unheard or unheeded. The land, the people, and life itself are all

seen by him in terms of his own ability to manipulate them. When Geoffry endangers his chance of going abroad to study for a career by making Clara McLeod, a city girl friend, pregnant, Weldon's reaction is predictable: "Nonsense! It is unfortunate that she's got pregnant as a result, but that's no fault of yours" (p. 124). He promptly, and with characteristic cynicism, arranges for an abortion (without the girl's knowledge) with the sophisticated, urbane, Eurasian family doctor:

"Oh!" Dr. Roy raised his brows and nodded slowly. "Begun to sow his wild oats, eh?"
"Like his father. Blood will out, Roy. What to do?"
They both laughed over the sally and Dr. Roy told a *risqué* story with child-birth as the theme. (p. 141)

The sterile, cynical worldliness of their conversation is given a further ironic twist when we learn later on that Geoffry's chosen career, like Dr. Roy's, is medicine. Although Big Man Weldon is the son of a mulatto mother and an English father, he is nevertheless presented as the stereotype of the imperialist pioneer in outlook and temperament—

Had he lived years and years ago in England he might have been a great general like the Duke of Wellington or Lord Clive of India, or a great sea-adventurer . . . like Drake or Frobisher or Raleigh. (p. 40)

—and he remains totally committed to a colonist's "external" view of the land as a means of wealth through conquest. Geoffry, however, inherits his father's "European," boldly outward-looking attitude as well as his mother's peasant sensibility. His education at an institution, run on English public-school lines (he and his friend Stymphy speak a "Billy Bunter" [20] sort of English), has helped only to widen the already present division within his consciousness, so that he is able to reject the land and the life of the peasants while recognizing at the same time that these things are a vital presence from which he is excluded:

"It's queer," Geoffry said slowly as if speaking to himself, "but at most times when I look upon scenes like this I get the feeling that I'm locked out. I want to feel deeply about beauty, but something in me always seems to say that it's not for me." (p. 79)

In fact, the character of Geoffry, and the significance of his relationship with Kattree, provide what is perhaps the most interesting
focal point in the novel, for he and Kattree are made to represent the
two parts of what later becomes a familiar dichotomy in Mittelholzer's work: Intellect/Spirituality *versus* Emotion/Sensuality. Kattree and her sister, Beena, are the embodiment of natural beauty and
goodness, as yet untainted by the outside world. They both reflect the
unselfconscious openness of the land itself:

> Beena was thin and very brown, like Ramgolall. She had beauty like the
> beauty of the savannah before the sun rose in the morning. Kattree was of
> a lighter brown and her eyes were like the dark lowing of the cows in the
> after-glow of sunset. (p. 8)

But it is Kattree who is made to function as a living symbol of the
savannah:

> Walking with grace in her dirty clothes, she looked like a figure created
> by the magic of the savannah and the sunlight. She looked aloof from the
> good and the evil of the earth, and yet a chattel of both. She looked se-
> rene like the far-reaching plain of stunted grass and earth. (pp. 34–35)

Geoffry is strongly attracted to the natural, physical vitality of Kattree and the Corentyne, but at the same time longs for the outer
world of ambition and culture. He tells her:

> "Your sort of life is the sort of life I want deep in me, but, of course, my
> ambitious and artistic longings upset everything. . . . I'd begin to dream
> of the cultured world beyond all this savannah and water, of London and
> symphony concerts. . . ." (p. 260)

This is, of course, the familiar, hackneyed theme of the conflict between Nature and Nurture, with Kattree in the role of Noble Savage;
but it is also a foreshadowing of what is now a much-discussed and
well-documented problem: the Caribbean artist's crisis of identity—
his need for roots within the context of his own landscape as well as
for the cultured, Metropolitan atmosphere in which his art can grow
and flower. It is a dilemma which still faces the Caribbean writer, and
makes possible the apparent paradox in which the successful Caribbean writers (with few exceptions) live and work abroad, mainly in
Britain, but quarry their material from within a Caribbean conscious-

ness. That the simple need for access to publishing houses (of which
there are still only a very few in the West Indies) was not by any
means the most important reason for the exodus of writers which began shortly after Mittelholzer's departure for England in 1948 is at-
tested to by the comments of the writers themselves.

In a radio discussion in 1963 between a group of Commonwealth
writers on the subject of the overseas artist living in London, Wilson
Harris gave this as his reason for "self-exile":

I came from Guiana because I had to gain a certain distance from the
stage where I wanted to set these novels—the novels of the Guiana
quartet. . . . I like the English landscape. . . . I find that this is an enormous relief after the harsh South American jungle . . . I mean it's stimu-
lating at one level but it's also—it has this claustrophobic character.[21]

Jan Carew, in another, earlier radio discussion, had rejected the idea
of a "return to one's roots . . . Africa or India or China or whatever
land one's ancestors came from," since "this as you know is very
difficult in the West Indian melting-pot"; and in the same discussion,
Denis Williams suggested a solution:

Certainly, the way out of this dilemma, it seems to me, doesn't lie in
turning back, but in facing the future—not in the absolute rejection of
Europe, but in knowing Europe better . . . once we succeeded in doing
this, then we can accept or reject what we will from this civilization.[22]

What most of the Caribbean writers seemed to have in common, in
the 1950s and early 1960s, at any rate, was the desire to "get out," as
Lamming puts it in *The Pleasures of Exile*,[23] to leave the Caribbean
so as to avoid the atrophy of creative talent which remaining might
bring about. V. S. Naipaul's nightmare, recalled by him when on a
return visit to Trinidad in 1960—

. . . For many years afterwards in England, falling asleep in bed-sitters
with the electric fire on, I had been awakened by the nightmare that I
was back in tropical Trinidad.[24]

—is a later expression of the same inner panic felt by Mittelholzer on
his return to his homeland in 1956. He too records a recurring nightmare: the feeling of being "trapped" by one's origins:

And then, with a shudder, I would awake to find myself in Bagshot, Surrey, or in Montreal, Canada, or on the Maxwell Coast of Barbados, and the relief would be tremendous.[25]

George Lamming had, in 1956, already recognized the dilemma of the Negro/Caribbean writer as a manifestation of a more universal *malaise*:

To speak of the Negro writer is therefore to speak of a problem of Man . . . of man's direct inner experience of something missing . . . a condition which is essentially . . . tragic.[26]

It is this sense of incompleteness, of "something missing," which tortures young Geoffry Weldon, as it had tortured his creator. In an early poem entitled "For Me—the Backyard," Mittelholzer expresses his disgust of polite collar-and-tie society which he rejects for the simple, more natural life of the Folk:

> . . . And why should I even spurn
> These little ragged clumps of fern
> And the rickety latrine standing near
> The old grey-trunked Tamarind!
> Assuredly for me—the naive backyard
> Where *bajak* ants, without hypocrisy, troop by
> And no gentlemen politely smile and lie.[27]

In "October Seventh," however, a sense of the inadequacy of the simple, "passional" life is clear:

> Yes in me I am troubled
> By some hungry want
> That stirs the hollow of me
> And will haunt
> Will haunt me long after
> This night with my passion
> This night that is warm and stilled
> Hath been brushed aside
> In my usual fashion
> With a smile and a chuckle
> —And my empty laughter.[28]

His short story "Sorrow Dam and Mr. Millbank" [29] is also centered around the conflict between a "civilized," urban way of life and the more natural, physical life of the peasants. The timorous bank clerk Mr. Millbank—a Prufrock figure who, on his nightly walks along "Sorrow Dam" on the New Amsterdam east coast, is attracted more and more to the simple, quietly happy life of the poor East Indian peasants—finally takes his fate into his own hands. The tongue-in-cheek story ends on a wry but pathetic note:

And Mr. Millbank, despite all that was said, despite all that everyone did to dissuade him, went and lived in the little cottage he had built. And he still lives there and works hard and wades barefooted through the rain to bring in his cows. Like any of the peasants. Himself a peasant. The silly madman.

Geoffry's crisis of identity, like Mr. Millbank's, embodies this split between two ways of life, but reveals at the same time another, more disturbing aspect—an inability to reconcile intellectual and physical urges. Against Kattree's unaffected sexuality his own guilt-ridden condition appears neurotic:

"There are so many things one would like to root oneself away from but just can't. Where sex is concerned especially, I can't help myself when it comes to sex. I'm like a piece of wood moving towards the centre of a whirl-pool. . . . In a way, the thought of sex irritates me. It seems so petty and contemptible. And yet it attracts me such a terrific lot that I can't do without it. That's what makes me want to commit suicide sometimes, you see." (p. 273)

A clear case, one suspects, of what D. H. Lawrence called "sex in the head." In fact it is this aspect of Geoffry's inner division which predominates and which is ultimately responsible for his cynicism and rootlessness. The suggestion in Louis James's introduction to the Heinemann edition that he is merely "sophisticated" or "ruthless" in his rejection of Clara McLeod or of Kattree misses both the fact that he feels deeply guilty and ashamed when Clara (who is, apparently, as "sophisticated" as he) goes through with the abortion without a murmur, and that he is too honest to mislead the simple, innocent Kattree into thinking that his affection for her has anything more than a sexual basis:

"I'm not in love with you yourself—only with your body. I told you that on the second day we were together, if you remember, and you said that

you were quite satisfied with my loving only your body. Ugh, but I'm sick
of loving bodies, Kattree. It leaves me unsatisfied and depressed." (p. 292)

He is capable, too, of self-criticism, and can admit the possibility that
"I may be nothing more than a great, conceited ass" (p. 293). In
Geoffry Weldon we can recognize the prototype of the virile Mittelholzer hero whose fear of spiritual atrophy leads to deliberate sexual repression and a preoccupation with occult science and Eastern
mysticism in an attempt to enter "into the pure spirit of the Higher
Plane." [30] The need to find a solution to the conflict between Flesh
and Spirit is the driving force behind Gregory Hawke of *Shadows
Move among Them* (1951), Hubertus van Groenwegel of *The Harrowing of Hubertus* (1954), Mr. Holme of *The Weather in Middenshot*
(1952), Brian Liddard of *A Tinkling in the Twilight* (1959), Garvin
Jilkington and Lilli Friedlander of *The Jilkington Drama* (1965), and
Sheila Chatham of *The Aloneness of Mrs. Chatham* (1965). Geoffry
Weldon is only the first of many Mittelholzer characters who, faced
with an almost irreconcilable inner division of consciousness, are
drawn "like a piece of wood moving towards the centre of a whirl-
pool" (p. 273).

The main presence in *Corentyne Thunder*, however, is not a human
one. It is the landscape itself, which remains an ever-present, enduring reality, indifferent to human conflict. As Ramgolall becomes a
more and more peripheral figure and Geoffry and Kattree come into
focus to give way in turn to the triangle of Sukra, Jannee, and Beena
and then that of Jannee, Beena, and Boorharry, so the brooding
savannah seems to enclose them all as they work, play, make love,
and die. Their lives are affected, whether they know it or not, by the
moods of the weather; and the weather is always close at hand. Almost every chapter begins or ends with a description of the weather,
about which there is some reference on almost every page. Human
character is often described in terms of the weather. Big Man Weldon
has a severe, forbidding manner, we are told:

Yet there ran in him a kindly vein, kindly like the golden vein of light
that one can sometimes see running along the horizon when all the sky is
heavy grey. (p. 41)

And Jannee's moody taciturnity conjures up in Beena's mind a natural image:

Jannee slowly knocked out his pipe and began to refill it, and Beena thought of a black cloud moving silently overhead in calm air. (p. 133)

She feels "as though lightning had flashed sharply and her soul were awaiting the deafening roar of the thunder" (p. 133). Even the one climactic incident in the novel—the brutal murder of Boorharry—is made to seem no more unnatural or sensational than the destruction of a coconut palm by lightning, an image with which the deed becomes associated in Jannee's mind:

When Beena told them of how the lightning had cut Manoo's coconut palm in half, Jannee grunted and muttered: 'Shoulda Boorharry 'e cut in half.' (p. 184)

The weather, the changing faces of the land, the way the rice grows inevitably toward the harvest: the real life and heart of the novel are *here*, one feels, and transitory human activity is deliberately distanced and tacitly commented upon by the slow, inexorable turning of the years. This, rather than Mittelholzer's limited view of Ramgolall's possibilities, is why *Corentyne Thunder* never really becomes the tale of a cow-minder it sets out to be and remains instead the evocation of a living landscape within which move a people with their own unique way of life.

The weather, for Mittelholzer, was a subject of lasting and almost obsessive interest, as his diaries show, and could affect him in an unusually direct, physical way. Thunderstorms, in particular, gave him a definite, sensuous thrill which he related in kind to the pleasure he derived from the music of Wagner, and it is significant that, in the unfinished "leitmotiv trilogy," he attempted to combine the elements of music, weather, and landscape by using "Wagnerian" *leitmotivs* (the phrase "thunder returning," in the novel of that name, is one of the *leitmotivs* used to suggest impending tragedy), many of which contain images of the weather and the natural environment. *The Weather Family* (1958), *Of Trees and the Sea* (1956), *The Weather in Middenshot* (1952) and that extraordinary Gothic ghost-story, *My Bones and My Flute* (1955), exemplify the technique through which Mittelholzer uses weather and landscape to inform and control his characters' behavior so that climate, natural environment, and human thought and action become inseparably welded together. The dark, menacing clouds over the Corentyne reappear as the gathering storm in the mind of the psychopath, Charles Pruthick (*The Piling of Clouds*, 1961) as surely as the lightning that "flashed sharply" in Beena's soul is followed by the later, internal thunder which draws together Richard and Lindy and almost precipitates a tragedy in *Thunder Returning* (1961) in which the hero, Richard Lehrer, can be seen as a more mature, more tortured Geoffry Weldon, now finally alienated from the land of his birth and from himself. The cry of the goatsucker, which in *Corentyne Thunder* is an integral but unremarkable feature of the landscape—

. . . And once a goat-sucker, lying flat on the road a little way ahead, said: "who-you?" and flew off in swift silence. (p. 172)

—is seen, in retrospect, as the first, perhaps unconscious, stirring of the theme of psychic division: the "zweideutigkeit" felt by the hero of *Uncle Paul* (1963), and, indeed, by Mittelholzer himself.

In fact, most of Mittelholzer's later themes are already present, in embryo, in *Corentyne Thunder*. Big Man Weldon's gruff, practical attitude to life, his rough, planter's philosophy—

The damned world wants re-organizing. That's what's wrong. Less talk about morality and religious myth and more simple, practical common-sense. (p. 124)

—is heard again in the later work, where (especially in the "English" novels) it acquires the compulsive, dogmatic tone which eventually led to the publishers' repeated rejection of Mittelholzer's work. The sense of the Guyanese past, of life on the old Dutch plantations and the legends born of a violent history of slavery, are present in the description of Dr. Roy's house, "Vryheid," which was "built in 1827 by a Dutch planter, Mynheer Vanderhyden, whose tombstone may still be seen in the backyard" (p. 139), and which is haunted by the ghost of a young, black slave who stands guard over the Dutchman's coffin and buried jar of gold coins. It is Mittelholzer's double sense of the violence and mystery of the past with its residues of legend and racial admixture that pervades the Kaywana trilogy and *My Bones and My Flute* (1955) and creates the charged, hallucinatory world of *Shadows Move among Them* (1952); but the intolerable, inner conflict of the individual—the division of consciousness which afflicts the young Geoffry Weldon, forcing him to consider suicide as the only possible solution—is the most notable (and the most disturbing) theme in *Corentyne Thunder*, and finally emerges as the central theme of the later novels.

The Kaywana trilogy[31] is generally accepted as Mittelholzer's most outstanding work. It is certainly the finest example of his ability to organize a wealth of detail (the time-span of the novels is approximately 337 years) in the telling of a story of epic proportions. To Mittelholzer, who identified with a Swiss/German ancestor[32] and felt a sense of "genetic damage," the sexual and racial conflict and the resultant mixing of "bloods" involved in the violent slave-past of Guyana, in which his ancestry actually took root, must have seemed a natural choice for what was to be his *magnum opus*. His love of storytelling, his sense of the mystery and excitement of the past, his ability to evoke the atmosphere and "feel" of a place, his delight in vigorous, often violently sensational action, his prodigious facility for inventing, amassing, and organizing detail all came together to equip him for the formidable task he set himself: the imaginative reconstruction of the social and political history of Guyana from the early seventeenth to the middle of the twentieth century, and, within this framework, the epic saga of the growth and development of the van Groenwegel family tree. Mittelholzer's diligent research and scrupulous honesty are apparent in the use he makes of the slim documentation available[33] and in the chronological accuracy of historical, factual events in the novels. Like *The Life and Death of Sylvia* (1953), the main theme of the Kaywana trilogy involves a working-out of the author's theories of "strength" and "weakness." Within the mazelike, winding corridors of "Huis Kaywana" runs the thread of "blood," the "strength" or "weakness" of which finally determines the character and actions of every member of this extraordinary family: and it is this theme, with its complex irony (a complexity which has generally gone unacknowledged or unnoticed by Mittelholzer's critics), that one can trace through these three novels.

The theme of the trilogy is announced at the opening of *Children of Kaywana* when Kaywana, who is half aboriginal Indian and "half English sailor" (p. 14), reveals her unalloyed pride in her English blood which sets her apart as "stronger" and more intelligent than the Indians, who appear childlike and foolish alongside her. Even Wakkatai, the shaman, who is an important figure—a leader among the Indians—is made to look little more than a superstitious, easily flattered, fraudulent character. August Vyfuis, the young Dutchman whose overtures are instantly acceptable to Kaywana, is presented, on the other hand, as the possessor of desirable qualities, among which "strength" is of primary importance:

"You're strong. I like the way you hold me . . . I like men so. . . . The others want me, but they can't even look at me in my eyes straight. They beg and plead. I don't like men to beg and plead. They must hold me and take me and show they have more strength than I have." (p. 12)

After the heroic death of August Vyfuis during a Spanish raid, Adriansen van Groenwegel comes on the scene. He too receives automatic approval from Kaywana, and for the same reason:

He had strength—like the strength of August. He was the kind of man, she felt certain, who would not plead with a woman. (p. 17)

Although Adriansen often insists that " 'I'm a hard man' " (p. 22), he nevertheless introduces a note of antiheroic "weakness" in his use of flattery and guile to get his own way, finally winning over even the hostile Wakkatai to his side. As he tells young August (the son of August Vyfuis):

"When we're up against the Wakkatais of this world, force is not the weapon to employ, my boy. The weapon is subtlety. . . ." (p. 42)

But at the same time Adriansen's attitude to his enemies, contrasted with Kaywana's implacable hatred (" '. . . When anyone hates me I hate in return. If anyone hurts me I hurt them in return . . .' " [p. 43]), is shown to be both more intelligent and more humane. When there is a threat of Indian revolt and Kaywana suggests that the soldiers be called out to quell any uprising by force, Adriansen says,

"Nothing of the sort. We must never threaten them with violence except as a last resort. These Indians are good people. It's always a mistake to show them force. . . . There are other ways of being strong than the way of guns, Kaywana." (p. 47)

And when the rebellion does take place, it is Adriansen's "weak" policy of tact which succeeds, and Kaywana's bravery (like August Vyfuis's) which is ultimately futile. The climactic fight between Kaywana and her children and the Indians led by Wakkatai is remembered later by Willem, one of the van Groenwegel children who survived (Kaywana and most of the other children perish in the fight) with a deep sense of pride:

"My mother was a fighter. Do you know what it is to have a mother who can stand up with her sons and fight to the death?" (p. 61)

But by then it has acquired an ironic flavor, since Willem himself would not have survived, had not Adriansen, by arguing with the rebels and appealing to their common sense—but showing no less bravery than Kaywana—managed to put down the rebellion even while Kaywana and Wakkatai were locked in mortal combat.

From the very first chapter, then, Mittelholzer's view of "strength" and "weakness" is seen to be, if not ambiguous, at least presented with a certain irony, an irony which grows in significance throughout the book, reaching its climax in the later chapters where Hendrickje attempts to establish the van Groenwegel family as a power in the land. Willem, meanwhile, is the "strong" character whose views are given the center of the stage. He reiterates the theme of "blood" *ad nauseam:*

"It's blood that counts, Griselda. Blood. Men can say we're van Groenwegels with the bar sinister. Let them say it. Not a mortal can drain the blood of that old man from my veins—or the veins of my children." (p. 61)

When Major Scott and his marauding band of Caribs attack the colony in 1666, Willem seizes the chance to prove the "strength" of van Groenwegel blood. His wife, Griselda, and his son, Reinald, are presented as "weak" elements: indeed, the "strong" and the "weak" are quite unmistakably labeled, as, for example, in Reinald's pitiful efforts to get his group of slaves to rally during the siege:

" . . . Don't you hear me? Please," besought Reinald. "Please. . . . For God's sake get back to your posts. . . . Quick! I beseech you! Quick!" None of them made any move to obey. (p. 86)

His brother Laurens has to come to his aid with a demonstration of the required "strength":

"Never speak kindly to slaves, or try to persuade them to do anything. . . . Take up your positions again and start firing as Massa Reinald directs you or I'll kill you. I mean it. I'll kill you, you black cowardly clumps of filth!" He trembled. He had an insane look. (p. 87)

The attack is successfully resisted, and Willem, swollen with what he now considers an amply justified sense of pride, casually dismisses the death of his "weak," academically minded brother Aert, who, it is reported, died retreating from the enemy "clutching two haversacks of books to his bosom as though they were beloved creatures" (p. 96):

"The soft fool. Reinald will be Aert all over again. A misty-brained book-worm. Anyway, there's Laurens. I have hope for that boy. I must build him up. I must consolidate him. He won't let me down." (p. 96)

Willem's remark, "The decades will show whether my faith in our blood was justified" (p. 96), embodies the ironic nature of the theme of these novels; for it is with Laurens's later introspective question-ings that the value of a credo of "strength" which excludes finer feel-ings such as unselfishness, respect, and love is examined and found wanting.

We are frequently shown Laurens's private thoughts on matters concerning family pride and his own attitude to it. In the big house at Cartabo Point (the scene of Kaywana's death) he is aware of being both attracted to and revolted by the family history and clearly disen-chanted with his father's insistence on the importance of "blood":

The family pride is on his brain. Susannah says it's a mania. He can think of nothing but our blood: our fire-blood, as he calls it. Our stand up the Mazaruni against Scott's Caribs has made him trebly pompous and ob-sessed with the importance of the family. (p. 98)

When his sister Susannah visits him, her advice on whether he should marry simply for the sake of carrying on the family name is balanced:

"Certainly not. Fall in love first. Your happiness comes before any such considerations as family survival. Not that you mustn't try to see that the name goes on. I do get a little throb of pride when I remember that I'm a van Groenwegel, but the idea can be overdone." (p. 101)

Laurens's attraction to his house-slaves, Hannah and Katrina; the bas-tard, mulatto girls who are the product of the young August's earlier excursions into the slaves' logies, is seen by him as "an instinctive partiality for coloured women . . . ," perhaps even "a degenerate streak" (p. 98)—another sign of "weakness." But this "weakness" is accompanied by a moral strength, since his sense of decency will not permit him to overcome his shyness with the girls by simply getting drunk and ravishing them as his fellow planters would. Susannah's remark, "Your morals are very high. I like you for it" (p. 110), seen in the context of the brutal sexual licence taken, as a matter of course, by the planters in their treatment of female slaves, is a compliment indeed. Laurens's own estimate of himself at this point, "He was soft. He was not a man" (p. 109), is, therefore, not without a certain irony. Katrina, the self-effacing, loyal slave-girl who becomes pregnant for him (and so introduces the "taint" of Negro blood into the family), unwittingly brings home to Laurens a moral lesson. When he suggests marriage, she reminds him with alarm of her position as a slave, and he replies, with a sudden realization of the truth:

"I don't care. To-night I'm seeing things differently. To-night I can see you as a human being. It doesn't matter how you speak—or that you wear a smock. You've broken down my pride. I see you now as a woman. You have my child in you, and you're good. You have a good nature." (p. 133)

This attitude comes from Laurens's recognition of precisely those deeper, human qualities beneath the surfaces of skin and family, and Willem's furious reaction to the "taint" introduced by this marriage—

"The bitterness of this day will never fade. I shall never be converted to the belief that our family has not been tainted. I shall never be reconciled to this slave-blood which Laurens has seen fit to introduce into our family." (p. 137)

—receives a sharp, ironic twist in the following chapter, for the child of this marriage, Hendrickje, grows up to be the ultimate embodiment of what Willem himself had always regarded as the van Groenwegel "fire-blood": a fierce, proud figure like Kaywana, imbued with an obsessive family pride, who institutes and enforces the motto, "The van Groenwegels never run!"

Hendrickje, a precocious, strong-willed child, begins quite early to demonstrate symptoms of extreme "van Groenwegelism." So concerned is she about the danger of "diluting" the strength of the family blood that, at the age of fifteen, she earnestly suggests to Ignatius van Groenwegel, her cousin, that they consider marriage so as "to keep the blood together" (p. 145). Dismissing their grandmother, Griselda, as a "weakling," she says with chilling intensity:

"She brought weak blood into the family. That musn't happen again. You must marry a girl with fighter-blood. A girl like me. Then we'll have hard children to carry on the tradition. We have to keep hard." (pp. 145–46)

This is the echo of Willem's own obsession, returning now with added power and virulence; and through Hendrickje, the mania for "strength" expresses itself with growing violence. She has a megalomaniac vision of the family spreading and becoming an irresistible force in the land, seeing herself as a fertile soil from which a whole race of hardy, ruthless van Groenwegels will one day spring. Riding roughshod over everyone in her path, including her father, Laurens, she inevitably gets her way. She has enormous confidence in the strength of van Groenwegel "blood," and in herself as its representative—

"The family, for me, will always come before everything else. . . . I have faith in myself. My spirit is strong, and my body is strong. I'm going to prove a good breeder. I'm hoping to have no less than ten children— twelve, if possible. More. And among these a few must be like me." (p. 178)

—this confidence is proved, however, like Willem's faith in van Groenwegel blood, to be unjustified. As the novel proceeds (in the chapter headed "The Way to Power"), Hendrickje's cold-blooded drive to establish herself as a sexually potent breeder of van Groenwegels is made to appear ridiculous, and, finally, grotesque. A kind of grossly fecund, tropical Lady Macbeth, she is ruthless toward all who get in her way, including her ineffectual, artistic husband, who is treated merely as a provider of the ancestral sperm and made to run the household and feed the baby while she rides out into the fields, whip in hand. Her vision of herself as a "born breeder," strong-willed and "physically invincible" (p. 187), suffers a rude shock, however, for she is able to have only two children, both of whom (thanks to her consistent brutality and lack of warmth) develop a lively hatred for their mother, one becoming homosexual—almost as a protest, one feels, against her own vicious sensuality—and the other eventually growing up to hate the idea of family pride. After a fall (sustained when, pregnant, she had insisted on riding out into the fields) she loses the third baby and is told that she will not be able to have any more children. She does become pregnant twice after this, but each time the baby does not survive long. Her strength of will— "I won't give up . . . I must and will have more children. By sheer will I'll conceive again" (p. 195)—is ultimately futile. In Mittelholzer's treatment of Hendrickje the excessive love of strength for its own sake and the unreasoning insistence of family pride are shown to be a form of willful self-delusion, as is Hendrickje's denial of a desperate, unfulfilled need for warmth and love:

"Love and tenderness can go. I'm prepared to live without them . . . so long as I have my children as planned, so long as I have them established in the country and the most powerful family, all else can go. . . ." But though she wrote this, the actuality was different. (p. 215)

Her "weak" husband, Ignatius, realizes that, for all her strength and cruelty, "in many ways; Hendrickje is a simpleton" (p. 204) and that "she's a tortured woman" (p. 221). Asked by his son, Adrian, whether his grandfather, Laurens, believes, as his mother does, that the family must be powerful at all costs, he replies: "No. . . . Your Grandfather Laurens is a balanced man, . . . It was your Great-Grandfather Willem who began this power campaign. But even he was not the fanatic that your mother is" (p. 217).

Adrian, however, suffers what is, in effect, a temporary attack of "van Groenwegelism"—the malignant effect of his inherited "blood" —in spite of the fact that his mind is already warped by hatred of his mother and all that she stands for. He finds himself revolted by his homosexual brother, Cornelis, and incestuously drawn to his mother, who, to his great consternation, appears "not such a bad person after all" (p. 239). This digressive episode, in the chapter headed "Oedipus," is used by Mittelholzer, one suspects, mainly as an occasion for propounding his own views on incest. Hendrickje says, with obvious authorial approval:

"Don't let's have illusions about ourselves. We're mother and son, but we're in love like two animals. We want to be in bed." (p. 255)

This view—that sexual urges are entirely physiological and therefore "natural," even if expressed in a taboo relationship such as incest— often encountered in Mittelholzer's work, is elaborated more fully in *The Harrowing of Hubertus* (1954). Here, it appears merely as an attempt at erotic sensationalism, since nothing is made of the episode and it is not used to advance the plot in any way, except to suggest that even Hendrickje, in need of human affection, can benefit from receiving it. Her long, intimate chats with Adrian certainly soften her brutal attitude to the slaves, who now receive larger rations and fewer whippings. The division of loyalties experienced by Adrian, however, who feels both a violent moral revulsion from, and a strong sexual attraction toward, his mother, is a notable example of the psychic imbalance deriving from mixed racial inheritance—the conflict that is to "harrow" the life of Hubertus in the second book of the trilogy.

When the French invade the colony and Hendrickje, like Willem, seizes the opportunity to demonstrate the family motto—"The van Groenwegels never run"—Adrian quietly pricks the balloon of her pride:

"I don't care one jot about our family traditions. . . . This family pride you've always tried to instil into us is nothing to me. I think it foolish and small—unworthy. Why should we consider ourselves better than other people? It's not right."

When the siege begins, Hendrickje, sitting disconsolately in her ruined bedroom, tearful and covered with the dust of battle, is an almost pathetic anachronism:

"I feel distracted, Adrian. Distracted. I didn't anticipate this. I thought they would have attacked with muskets—as in '66. I didn't reckon with bombs." (p. 272)

Adrian's bravery is not in question, for he does stay on to resist the attack, which nevertheless ends in defeat for the van Groenwegels. The slaves desert ("Missy never treat us good. Why we should stay in house and fight for her?" [p. 273]), Cornelis runs away with a French turncoat friend, and as Adrian calmly calls back the French envoy whom Hendrickje had sent away with a grandiose show of defiance, the whole myth of van Groenwegel "strength" is seen to be hollow. Adrian vows that

"In future one of the things I shall work for is to destroy the memory of the old days and the deeds of our ancestors. . . . I shall live to wipe it away, to poison the minds of my children against it." (p. 279)

As the novel moves toward the great slave rebellion of 1763, Hendrickje degenerates completely, becoming a monster of cruelty, burying alive a sick, old slave so as to create more space in the logies, and dabbling in obeah with Bangara, her favorite head-slave and paramour. Rosaria, a dissolute half-Spanish, half-Carib slave-girl, is deliberately used by Hendrickje as a means of furthering the van Groenwegel line, since Jabez (the only other healthy van Groenwegel male, apart from Adrian), who is Rosaria's husband and the father of Hubertus, is beaten up and suffers castration at the hands of a jealous rival. Adrian, unaware of her plan, obligingly fathers, with Rosaria's eager help, a brood of mulatto van Groenwegels, in the mistaken belief that he is hurting his mother's pride in the family's "blood." Adrian himself, now totally unbalanced by hatred, becomes a mere cipher, and dissoluteness reigns. "Better dissolute animals," says Hendrickje as she encourages the lowest urges and the worst vices of the children (in a ghastly *reductio ad absurdum* of her policy of "hardening" them), "than high-thinking dreamers" (p. 329). Among the sensational occurrences that follow are the burning alive of Bangara, the attempted murder of Hendrickje by Rosaria, and the latter's death at the hands of her own children who, from a vantage point in a tree, shoot her down in the home of her latest lover. Amid all the lust and carnage and childish avowals of loyalty to the van Groenwegel code of "honor"—intended as a mordant comment on Hendrickje's philosophy of "strength" as the answer to life's haphazard brutality, and not simply as erotic or sadomasochistic titillation (although this element is always present)—the one silent voice is that of Jacques, who instinctively hates cruelty and rejects the amoral, brutish philosophy of Hendrickje and the rest. When the rebellion of 1763 takes place, Lumea's earlier remark,

"There will never be any slave uprising in this colony. . . . They haven't got the guts—nor the intelligence—to marshal themselves into a fighting force." (p. 397)

is seen to be ironic,[34] as is the young Laurens's contemptuous rejection of his in-laws, the Teuffers, as "weak" when he hears of the cowardice of Vincent Teuffer (whose mother was a van Groenwegel):

Laurens pawed the floor *with his deformed foot* and scowled. "That's why," he said, "we've got to be careful whom we pick for wives." (p. 397, my italics)

Laurens's misshapen foot is an outward sign of the dreadful, inner deformity imposed on them all by Hendrickje's insane will. Hendrickje herself appears almost senile with glee, tittering and cackling at the prospect of the impending fight. Jacques, who is captured by the rebel slaves and held hostage, functions as an objective observer of the scene. We witness the brutality of both sides through his eyes, and when his fear of physical pain (although, morally, he is not a coward) forces him to appeal to the rebel leader's sense of decency, Mittelholzer uses the situation to make a deftly ironic thrust:

> "Decency! *My* sense of decency!" Cuffy laughed. He backed away a pace or two and looked at Jacques. "You expect me to have decency! You look on me a black man, van Groenwegel, and talk about decency! Where I could get decency from?" (p. 450)

And when Amelia says of her black captors, "They're beasts. Beasts," Jacques replies, "Not more so than the beasts we have been toward them" (p. 447). The wheel comes full circle in the final chapter, headed "Finale: Like Kaywana," where, as in the beginning, the van Groenwegel family, led by a fanatical warrior-woman, faces the enemy. Jacques, who has escaped his captors, returns to the beleaguered family but finds that the rot has set in. With the exception of Hendrickje, they all want to give up the struggle and escape while there is still time. Jacques, disillusioned with the apparent senselessness of a world in which brutality seems the norm of human behavior, has come prepared to face certain death. His action is misunderstood by Hendrickje, whose delighted approval is the book's final irony:

> "Jacques, I'm beginning to feel that despite your softness, you are the hero among us."
> Jacques laughed. "Wrong, old lady. I wasn't born to be a hero. Heroes are strong. I'm one of the weak who have discovered the depressing truth that it takes strength to make a secure world. *Physical as well as moral strength*." (p. 507, my italics)

With the suggestion that a *balance* is needed for true, creative strength, the novel ends as they all meet their deaths resisting the inevitable.

Mittelholzer, in a letter to a friend, described *The Harrowing of Hubertus* as a "quiet book devoted chiefly to a study of the character of Hubertus van Groenwegel," who, he said, was "a projection of a facet of my own personality." [35] This, the second novel of the trilogy, opens, therefore, not with the theme of "strength" *versus* "weakness," but with a more personal, though allied, theme: the need for a coexistence of the two sides of one's personality—the physical and spiritual "selves." Hubertus, like so many of Mittelholzer's characters, is keenly aware of the fact that he is not an integrated being, that he suffers from a "division of consciousness":

There were times when Hubertus believed that he possessed another self over which he had no control. It caused him to do and say things he would normally have hesitated to do and say. It sprang surprises on him. Yet he knew that he approved of this self; he did not regret its presence. (p. 17)[36]

This suggests a psychological approach and prepares the reader for the low-keyed, introspective theme of self-discovery. Hubertus's awareness of an unpredictable, inner "self" *which he accepts* as a necessary counterpart of his outward, ego-personality is, in itself, an indication of psychic health. By his conscious approval of this "submerged" self, Hubertus apparently chooses the hard path of self-integration, the danger of which lies in the "swamping" nature of the Unconscious. Superficially, his struggle is simply between "low urges" and "high principles": between Flesh and Spirit; but, at a deeper level, it is also the conflict between the Ego and the Unconscious; and Hubertus's "harrowing" carries overtones of a universal, archetypal significance. According to C. G. Jung, the "inner voice"

. . . makes us conscious of the evil from which the whole community is suffering, whether it be the nation or the whole human race. But it presents this evil in an individual form, so that one might at first suppose it to be only an individual characteristic. . . . *But if we can succumb only in part, and if by self-assertion the ego can save itself from being completely swallowed, then it can assimilate the voice.* . . . (C. G. Jung, The Development of the Personality; No. 17 of *Collected Works*, Routledge & Kegan Paul, Ltd., 1954, p. 185, my italics)

Hubertus's "harrowing" can be regarded as an "individualized" form of the general guilt of the community of slave-owners and of the van Groenwegels in particular. Certainly the above quotation might serve almost as a summary of Hubertus's attempt at self-knowledge. He does "succumb only in part" to his willful, unpredictable "inner self," but avoids the danger of psychic disorientation and manages to achieve a precarious balance between his opposed "selves."

The problem expresses itself as an ambiguity of attitude, seen first as he considers the question of providing the aborigines with rum:

It was against his principles to give rum to Indians. Drunkenness, he was convinced, was impious . . . displeasing to the Almighty. Yet . . . to have adhered to his principles . . . would have meant that his family would have to do without game and fish, and; of greater importance, his slaves would have been more difficult to control. (p. 16)

Hubertus's dilemma reflects the double standards of the early European settlers and colonizers (who, it is said, "first fell upon their knees and then upon the aborigines"), for, faced with the choice of remaining loyal to his Christian principles or of jettisoning his religious scruples in order to maintain the *status quo*, he chooses the latter and, quite confidently, prays for divine forgiveness: "God," argued Hubertus, "was a reasonable Being" (p. 17). Within this concept of "loyalty," which he has chosen as a secure frame of reference for his actions, the double standard is made explicit:

Loyalty, felt Hubertus, was what mattered most in life. One must be loyal to God and Christian men and women. . . . The negro slaves and the Indians he considered as beings in an entirely separate category. . . . One did not have to be loyal to slaves and Indians. (p. 20)

Even in the matter of family pride, his "two-ness" expresses itself and sets the pattern of the duality which characterizes all his actions:

Our name? Proud of it? Van Groenwegel? . . . I don't want to remember how close I am to them in blood. It makes me feel tainted, too. . . . It is because of them—and their foul mother—that I have such low urges. . . . And now you tell me you're proud of the name. I can't understand that. . . . Yes, I can. That's the terrible part, my dear. I can. I'm proud of the name myself, though I spit at you for saying you are. (p. 83)

This suggests the schizoid tendency (a tendency of which Mittelholzer was himself victim) which appears as one of the main themes in most of Mittelholzer's serious work. The exploration of the sexual and emotional drives which influenced the actions of earlier van Groenwegels had revealed "strengths" and "weaknesses" which were the result of chance genetic transference and, as such, entirely outside the realm of moral choice. Hubertus, whose mania for consistence and control—for some fixed, external standard of reference—is mocked at every turn by the ambiguous nature of his own, inner disharmony, also, at first, chooses heredity as a suitable, culpable agent of control:

It is the mad beast in me. It defeats my restraint when I least expect it to. I'm sure I have inherited it from my mother, that lost woman, that pit of evil. Yes, evil. *She* was evil . . . some mysterious intuition informed me of it—since I was a boy. Evil, evil. (p. 71)

But whereas in *Children of Kaywana* (1952) brutality and dissoluteness are presented as the inevitable result of a credo of "strength" for its own sake and part of the general climate of the early slave plantations, in this novel they reflect and comment on the inner conflict of the main characters. When, for example, Hubertus sentences a slave to a particularly severe punishment for a petty misdemeanor, he is externalizing his self-torture:

Faustina rose, deciding that she must act. She must go and speak to him. It was not the man he was sentencing to this torture; it was himself. He would writhe on the broken bottles, not the man. (p. 86)

Similarly, the young Edward's cruel streak ("People to me are like pebbles. I always feel like kicking them along the ground" [p. 179]) stems from his detached, almost clinical view of human relationships, and his revulsion from sexuality. Like his cousin Hubertus, he has to learn to come to terms with his own, hidden nature; and the "buzzing as of a nest of desperate bees" (p. 279) within him is an image of the Unconscious seeking expression—an image that recurs in the later work and is used in *Latticed Echoes* (1960) and *Thunder Returning* (1961) as a leitmotiv for the brooding, insecure Richard Lehrer.

Throughout the novel, Hubertus tries to come to terms with his lack of psychic "wholeness" but derives little comfort from his reading of Spinoza's *Ethics* and St. Augustine:

That the fleshly in us can only be related to evil. This is foolish! Absurd! It is contrary to all one's instincts. . . . Moreover, I feel that we are born with tendencies for good or evil. It is the blood in us that dictates our allegiance to God or to the Devil. (pp. 118–19)

Hubertus's conviction that any deed is moral or immoral only in relation to the "allegiance" of the doer—whether inspired by genuine
("good") or corrupt ("bad") feeling—makes possible his adultery with
his cousin Faustina in spite of his own avowed, high principles. And it
is also this intuition that lies behind his apparently inconsistent attitude to the rebellious slave, Danrab, whom he pardons after having
ordered his severe punishment for the serious crime of sedition.

The description of the incident clearly implies that a sense of genuine, moral dignity attaches to the slave's "disloyal" action, which is
therefore worthy of respect:[37]

A black human being with character. Watching him from upstairs, Luise
felt almost as much awe for him as she did for her father. . . . He's a
slave and his skin is black but he is a man, she thought. If he were free
and had a house like this I could respect him. (p. 145)

Just as Hubertus's own "division of loyalties" finally sabotages all his
earlier attempts at an uncompromisingly Christian stance; so too the
problem of the incompatibility of Spirit and Flesh, first stated in an
apparently definitive way—

The flesh is not of necessity evil, yet to yield to its urges is to wound the
spirit. The spirit cannot grow in stature while the flesh is being satiated.

—undergoes a change, eventually leading to the less manichean view
of the older, sadder, and wiser Hubertus:

I used to think of God as an austere Spirit whose one purpose was to
punish mankind when the flesh triumphed, and scatter rewards when the
spirit showed its superiority. Now . . . well, now I am doubtful what my
conception is, because I have changed my attitude to the flesh. . . .
Surely if we can find good in human passion—the flesh—there must be
some element of the spirit contained in fleshly indulgence? (p. 270)

In fact, Hubertus's ultimate humanism ("You ask about God. Sometimes, my boy, I want to believe that I myself am God" [p. 270])
reflects his unwillingness to accept finally that any external agency,
such as heredity, should be held answerable for one's inconsistencies.
Even the narrow concept of loyalty to "blood," to the family, or to
the nation gives way to a more liberal view:

Look at the number of changes we have suffered since 1781. From Dutch to English then to French then back to Dutch now English again. What do nations matter, Bentley! Why can't we be loyal to each other as members of the human species. (p. 293)

This is a far cry from the early, narrow jingoism of the van Groenwegels and points the way to later novels, like *The Wounded and the Worried* (1962) and *The Aloneness of Mrs. Chatham* (1965), in which the problem of emotional balance and the need to transcend petty, conventional concepts of society are given a much wider significance.

One's impression that the theme of psychic integration is Mittelholzer's main concern in the novel is sustained by his treatment of other main characters who seem to function as negatively or positively charged complements, often appearing as the paired elements of a dichotomy. Rosalind Maybury, Hubertus's English wife, can be regarded as the spiritual, "sanctified" opposite of Faustina, his sensual, illicit mistress (who is also his cousin, and therefore doubly "taboo"); and Hubertus unites, in loving both women, his "sacred" and "profane" urges. His adultery with Faustina is not, therefore, simply an indulgent, sexual excess, but the necessary counterpart of his love for Rosalind, and contributes to the "balance" which he strives to maintain. He describes his feelings for both Rosalind and Faustina[38] as "deep and sincere" (p. 172) and does not regard his openly adulterous relationship with his cousin as immoral, since "so long as love is deep and sincere, whether the predicants or the law officials approve it or not, such love is a joy in God's sight" (p. 172). Hubertus's daughter, Luise, who has a sensitive, easily impressionable nature, is portrayed as a foil to the insensitive, cynical Edward, ten years her junior. She follows him around, a faithful, loving shadow, absorbing his cruelty, encouraging his talent for sketching (a sign of "weakness" in earlier van Groenwegels, but recognized by her as the valuable gift it is), and finally helping him to understand and accept their parents', and their own, sexuality. With the introduction of Clara Hartfield, the sensual equivalent of Faustina, the *ménage à trois* of Edward/Luise/Clara functions almost as a subplot to the relationship of Hubertus, Rosalind, and Faustina. Hubertus's marriage survives his infidelity largely because of Rosalind's Christian forbearance; but Luise, as Edward's wife, is able to rise above sexual jealousy, recognizing that Edward's love for her is not diminished by his physical desire for Clara. Edward, too, is more successful than Hubertus in

keeping a "balance" while accepting the fact that his moral principles are not proof against the irrational nature of his sexual urges.
Like Hubertus, who refuses to "deceive myself about myself" (p.
269), Edward is committed to personal integrity ("I am myself,
Clara. . . . I can't escape from myself" [p. 273]), and his own attempt to discover some unalterable Truth about himself and his relationships with others, mirrors and confirms Hubertus's. He says to
Clara,

"Cousin Hubertus is right. It's not easy to tell where the flesh ends and
the spirit begins. These afternoons with you have been beautiful. It wasn't
simply lust. There was the beauty of the spirit in them." (p. 277)

At the end of the novel, as the questioning cry of the goatsucker returns with its suggestion of the need to explore one's identity—

"Listen! A goatsucker. Such a long time I haven't heard one." . . .
Hoo-yoo!
   They listened, and it came again. Far away amidst the trees. Hoo-yoo!
(p. 294)

—we see the old Hubertus, still victim of his divided nature, but no
longer in any doubt of the need to find a solution from within *himself*:

". . . Do you still believe in God?"
"God. A Supreme Being. . . . Yes. Yes, Edward—I believe—have always believed—in myself." (p. 303)

Such, then, is the outline of the deeper, psychological theme of
psychic orientation which, first sounded in *Corentyne Thunder*
(1941), was to become the main theme of many of the later novels.
   Mittelholzer's handling of this psychological theme—his "character study" of Hubertus—is disappointingly superficial, however. The
reader is never allowed, so to speak, to observe the characters from
the inside; and attempts at describing inner feelings and emotions
tend to trail off into vagueness. Faustina's feelings, when she is out
walking with Hubertus, are generalized as "the uncertainties and
fluctuations of the warm mist that was the physical in her" (p. 71);
and Luise, fearing a return of Edward's earlier, childhood cruelty,
feels "a shrinking and shrivelling, as though a cold rag had brushed
her heart and it was her heart that was shrinking and shrivelling." (p.

196). Flattered by Edward's attentions, however, she feels "like a ghost contained in a cloud of love" (p. 178). When Edward's detached, artist's interest in Clara takes on a more personal tone, we are told that "a mist wreathed in his senses" (p. 267). This apparent ineptitude of style makes it difficult for the characters' inner conflict to emerge as a genuine struggle; nor is the writing free from a certain obvious sentimentality. An example of this is Faustina's rapturous memory of her sexual experience with Hubertus:

Oh, I wonder. And I wonder if she has even once tasted with Hubertus such bliss as I have done. I hope she has—once, twice, innumerable times. . . . Poor creature. I have robbed you, but I am a thief unrepentant. . . . Oh, sweet wet leaves! Lovely damp rain! (p. 97)

There is also what appears to be an attempt at erotic illustration for its own sake. Luise, asked by Edward to strip for a nude sketch, is too shy to do so; but when he reveals his wish to marry her, she relents and offers herself to him sexually. "When we're married," he says, "not before" (p. 184). The reader is thus prepared for a later, less inhibited sexual encounter; and, later on, when Luise again sits for him she undresses, and, predictably, tries to break down his reserve. Edward refuses, with great effort, to indulge in sexual intercourse, but is so excited that he nevertheless has an ejaculation. "Next time," promises Luise, "it will be different" (p. 192). These incidents (like the affair between Luise's sister Jacqueline and the Scots overseer, Robert Guire) are intended to illustrate the "unnaturalness" of a code of ethics which sanctions sexual intercourse only within marriage; but they function, one feels, mainly to provoke sexual excitement. But perhaps the most distracting element in the writing is the lack of restraint shown by Mittelholzer in bringing in extraneous, personal "theories," such as the innate masochism of women (a prominent feature in *Sylvia*, 1953), and of the efficacy of "doing *first* unto one's enemies as they would like to do to you." The former "theory" lies behind Luise's meek, almost grateful acceptance of Edward's cruelty, while the latter is expressed in Hubertus's "strong" attitude toward a possible slave uprising:

The strong, the ruthless win. The weak, the timid, the kindly and faltering are annihilated. . . . No, Rosalind, we must love our enemies—but when our enemies attack us we must butcher them without mercy. Or *we* shall get butchered. (p. 142)

The suspicion that this is only a self-conscious posturing is borne out by Hubertus's merciful treatment of the slave, Danrab, and his inability, at the last moment, to fire point blank into the face of a black attacker. In fact, neither "theory" is used structurally or thematically to advance the novel 'as a whole. To make matters worse, Mittelholzer is, it seems, unable (or unwilling) to follow his psychological theme through to its deeper implications. It is as if a powerful superego stands guard against too close an examination of "a facet of my own personality": that the subject—the need for psychic integration—was to close to his own psychological *malaise*. Hubertus's intuition that his "animal" self is as important to total psychic health as his "spiritual" self is never allowed to develop into a dialogue between Ego and Unconscious: "At this point Hubertus would think no further. He felt it would be an act of blasphemy to probe deeper into the mysteries" (p. 54). The novel fails ultimately as a work of art not because of ethical or moral superficiality, but because Mittelholzer does not explore the implications of his theme deeply enough, and so fails to create what might have been (and what the author apparently intended to be) a genuine psychological drama, a reconciliation of the opposing elements of the "Old Blood" within the alembic of Hubertus's consciousness.

Hubertus (1954), then, is the digressive book of the trilogy: a more personal novel, the main theme of which is the need for psychic integrity—a theme taken up again in later novels. It is in *Kaywana Blôod*, the final book of the trilogy, that Mittelholzer's examination of the "strengths" and "weaknesses" which stem from the "Old Blood" [39] takes its full, ironic effect. The first chapter contrasts the attitudes of Storm van Groenwegel's sons, Graham and Dirk, toward the family's traditions. Very soon, we find that Graham has inherited the "soft streak" and Dirk the "fire-blood"; and, while Graham develops an instinctive liking for dark-skinned people and a precocious, introspective nature, Dirk reveals a streak of cruelty, a surplus of family pride and Negrophobia. He appears almost to be a reincarnation of Hendrickje, complete with driving egotism and power-lust; and, like Hendrickje, he is allowed to damn himself by his own excesses in the name of "strength." The killing of a pet puppy for use as bait during an alligator hunt, is, for him, a rational act:

"All life is cruel," snapped Dirk. "And sometimes you have to be ruthless to achieve some big thing. . . . The capture of an alligator was more important than the life of a mere puppy." (p. 70)[40]

His mania for keeping the family "pure-blooded," and his consequent attempts to disengage the "colored" from the "pure" stock (even insisting that "mixed" van Groenwegels undergo a change of name), strenuously refusing to admit any Negro "taint" into the family, are shown, in the light of the earlier novels, to be a self-damaging preoccupation—the unhappy result of poring over the letters in the old canister, now the only link with the family's past. Dirk's "strength," presented as characteristic of the "Old Blood" in its forceful expression—

These slaves need a kick or thump now and then to keep them active. They are too lazy. . . . It would be a mistake to treat them like human beings. (p. 61)

—is, however, essentially comic, since it is clear that the old order is already dead. When the old slave, Cushy, is ordered by the young "massa" to relate what he recalls of the glorious van Groenwegel stand in 1763, his recounting of the sober facts of the rebellion upsets Dirk's romantic image of his ancestor's heroism: and when Cushy retreats to his logie to shelter from the sudden downpour, the grave "crisis of authority" which presents itself to Dirk's mind is used by Mittelholzer for purposes of ironic humor:

"I order you to come back out, Cushy!" Jacob growled.
"Don't be foolish, Dirk. You getting wet. Come in." . . . Dirk advanced a pace. "I shall strike you, Cushy! Do you hear me? Obey me this instant and come back out here. I won't enter your stinking logie."
Jacob laughed. "Stop all that talk, Dirk. It's my grandpa." (p. 66)

The incident finally resolves itself as an expression of the childish fantasy which, in effect, it is: and as Dirk and his colored half-brother, Jacob, run back to the house they play a game of "let's pretend":

"Let's imagine we're after a party of rebels in 1763. We're tracking them to their headquarters through the pouring rain. We're defying the elements because we're two brave van Groenwegels who won't be scared by God, man, or dirty slaves. What do you say?" (p. 67)

Dirk's sheer energy, however, is clearly intended as an admirable quality: "He's quite off his head," says his grandfather, "but he has spirit, damme!" (p. 67). His misfortune is that he is unable to harness it to good ends.

On the other hand, Graham, who is, significantly, put in charge of *Huis Kaywana*, determines to use his influence for the benefit of others:

I must prove what kindness and gentleness and consideration for one's fellow humans can bring forth. . . . I shall use my softness wisely. (pp. 102–03)

Graham's "softness" does, however, have its unfortunate counterpart: a view of sexual love as a comforting, sentimental indulgence. This is a genuinely "weak" trait which later develops into homosexuality, but he is nevertheless presented in the novel as a worthy successor to Hubertus. As Clara Hartfield puts it, "You are going to be an outstanding van Groenwegel—perhaps as outstanding as Cousin Hubertus" (p. 105). Graham's treatment of his slaves is humane; and it is surely ironic that the first chapel built for the slaves in the colony is established right at the heart of the "Old Blood"—plantation Kaywana—where Dirk later admires Hubertus's portrait, assuming his ancestor to be the possessor of outstanding qualities of "strength." The disabusing which follows is only another of the ways in which Dirk's obsession is quietly mocked:

"There's a man, by God! . . . There's a van Groenwegel to boast of!" Graham smiled slyly. "He used to curse the Old Blood. He called it the blood of beasts." (p. 160)

Later, when Dirk notices a large Bible on the table he says, condescendingly: "I suppose you read it every day. How Cousin Hubertus' ghost must sneer at you!" (p. 163). Graham informs him, with relish, that the Bible had, in fact, belonged to Hubertus. Again and again, Dirk's solipsism blights his relationships with others. His estimate of his colored half-brother, Jacob, as "lazy-minded" is shown to be hopelessly inaccurate; for it is Jacob who provides the momentum for Dirk's prosperous timber business:

Jacob, despite his air of indolence and apparent lack of ambition, was a man of ideas, and always on the alert for opportunities to improve the business. (p. 243)

Dirk's crude attempt to deflect Graham from marriage with Rose—a mulatto relative—fails, and he has to be content with Graham's agreeing to adopt the name of "Greenfield":[41] the English equivalent of Groenwegel. But Rose proves to be a fine, spirited individual, in spite of her "tainted" blood, and, later on, Dirk "would nod and tell himself that she had earned her place of honor in the history of the van Groenwegels" (p. 328) as mistress of *Huis Kaywana*. The reader is, however, also shown Rose's "weak" side: a sensual streak which rapidly develops as Graham becomes more and more "unmanly." Her long-standing attraction to Dirk, whose Negrophobia begins to dwindle, leads first to adultery with him (she has a child by him which is stillborn) and then, her longing for a child and for Dirk's love frustrated, to a *liaison sexuelle* with Pelham van Groenwegel. She dies in a fire after a rum-soaked orgy which is clearly an expression of her death-wish: "The flames had not hurt her, for she had given herself to them" (p. 328). She remains, like Hubertus, an enigmatic figure: an unstable mixture of "sacred" and "profane" elements.

Dirk's violent racial prejudice—the expression of his fear of genetic "taint"—is given an almost pathological significance; and it is this revulsion for "black blood" which underlies his treatment of Rose:

Black, shiny faces in the hot noonday sun. Frizzy black hair, in mops on their heads. To think of future van Groenwegels inheriting some of that pigment. And that coarse, rough, kinky hair! Never! Never! (p. 208)

This fear is shown, however, to be the result of a pathetic, personal fallacy, for Rose is the only woman (as Dirk admits) who "treats me with entire freedom and easy friendship and does not show towards me any hostility" (p. 139). Because of his deep, irrational fear of racial "impurity" (a fear that is deeply ironic, since he is unaware that Hendrickje, whose memory he venerates, is part Negro) he tries to distance her as he had distanced his boyhood friend, Jacob: but his superior manner disguises an inner instability,

. . . for in Rose's presence he was always unsure of himself; deep within, he knew why, but it angered him to admit it openly to himself. Secretly he feared Rose. (p. 134)

He forces himself to reject Rose's freely offered love (although he admits that he loves her) because she represents "black blood" and therefore the "soft streak" in the family; but immediately afterwards he cold-bloodedly forces the desirable Cornelia (whom he later marries) to have intercourse with him. His use of sheer physical strength to overcome the "white" Cornelia's reservations, and his stubborn refusal to give in to the "black" Rose's entreaties constitute an ethical perversion. Dirk's seduction of Cornelia is a crudely erotic, humorous, mock-heroic event, used by Mittelholzer, one suspects, to satirize Dirk's prowess as a "hard" van Groenwegel:

> ". . . Come on, warrior-woman. Yield."
> "Release me. This is absurd—and undignified. You are a madman."
> "It's a fight to the end. The van Groenwegels never run. And I'm Dirk—the hardest of them all." (pp. 157–58)

In this encounter, a ludicrously incongruous echo of earlier, heroic confrontations, not only is Dirk's "strength" made to appear questionable; but the predatory quality with which it is associated is also imaged in the harsh barking of a raccoon in the nearby bushes:

> The raccoon hack-hacked in the bush across the canal, getting nearer, now getting more distant, then getting nearer. On the prowl. (p. 157)

When, however, Rose lies dangerously ill after an abortive pregnancy, it is Dirk who encourages her will to live; and the rallying cry of the van Groenwegels is seen here to have a beneficial effect, for Rose finds the strength to recover. Mittelholzer is clearly at pains to suggest that qualities of strength and weakness are to be judged only insofar as they reflect, in a positive or negative way, deeper, humane values. Graham's "weakness" is praiseworthy when it expresses his innate belief in the finer qualities of the human heart: "I shall prove to Dirk that it isn't only hardness and brutality that can win power and glory for a family" (p. 102). And Dirk's "strength" is evil when, motivated by a mental image of power—the desire to "aim at the pinnacles" (p. 155)—it ignores the inner "essence" of things in its ruthless attempt to consolidate material benefits and to bolster narrow pride. In a rare moment of self-revelation, Dirk admits that his strength of will has become a prison:

> Yours is a flexible strength, Rose. Mine, alas, is brittle. I must be strict in the guard I place over my integrity, over my code of stability, for damage done to it—and this would be serious damage—would be irreparable. (p. 260)

Moreover, the "iron in his soul" (p. 155) is harnessed to an anachronistic dream of power. As Cornelia tells him, somewhat wryly,

"You were born too late, Dirk. You should have been a brother of those on the upper reaches in 1763. Then you would have had so many opportunities to kill and to be cruel." (p. 153)

The section of the novel which deals with the development of young Francis, Dirk's favorite nephew, appears, at first sight, to be simply another example of the author's penchant for lurid, sensational writing. The boy, left in charge of the younger children, suddenly reveals an unhealthy delight in bullying, indulging in obscene practical jokes and entering into grotesque, sexual experiments with the Negro slave, Elvira, who has encouraged him under the pretext of teaching him the secrets of *obeah*. Francis terrifies the other children with his disgusting behavior and lewd threats and when, finally, he realizes that Elvira has merely used him as a means of obtaining the money she requires to purchase her freedom he strangles her. Undoubtedly, Mittelholzer does give free rein to his own gift for bizarre storytelling and clearly panders to the public's enduring interest in the salacious; but this episode, like the one in which Mary offers herself to a coarse seaman to be ravished and defiled, is also used as a comment on the baneful effect of the canister with its burden of old letters which have already exerted so damaging an influence on Dirk's character. Francis says to Elvira,[42] during one of their perverted rituals,

"Cousin Dirk will discover that he isn't the most powerful van Groenwegel, after all. *All those letters he made me read about Grandma Hendri[ckje] and her cruelties—* . . . Wait until I begin to be cruel!" (pp. 351–52, my italics)

Later, he pleads with his uncle:

"It's those letters, Cousin Dirk. . . . I kept remembering what Grandma Hendrickje said. The pinnacles—and power. I was determined that I would win for myself all the power I could, so that I could take the family to the pinnacles—that's why I fell in with Elvira." (p. 355)

Dirk's "education" of Francis, his determination to "see that Francis made something of himself as a van Groenwegel" (p. 356), receives a horribly ironic fulfillment, in the face of which Cornelia's disclaimer that "he was born with a bad streak" (p. 357) appears, to say the least, disingenuous. The malignant influence of the "Old Blood" is acknowledged by Dirk in the final chapters of the novel:

I have spoiled so many lives by the words I've uttered. Between myself
and that canister, I wonder which has brought more unhappiness to the
van Groenwegels this past half century? (p. 477)

And when the last surviving letters (Laurens's to Susannah in the
seventeenth century) are unearthed and translated, Dirk discovers a
bitter truth about the "Old Blood." As he talks to himself, he fancies
that Rose's spirit is listening:

"The final irony, my love. Grandma Hendrickje's mother was a
quadroon—a *mestee*. . . . She had black blood in her, Rose, the queen of
the van Groenwegels. After Kaywana, our greatest heroine. An octaroon,
Rose. One eighth negro." (p. 497)

The irony is intensified by the fact that a number of the lower-class
colored folk in the novel are shown to be better mannered and to
possess higher principles than the upper-class whites and near-
whites. Dirk, supported by his parents, had insulted Rose and her
mother and a friend, Clara Hartfield, in his blind opposition to
Graham's wish to marry Rose. During the shocking display of crude
racial prejudice and vulgar social snobbery, Mrs. Clark, Rose's colored mother, "was the only one who had retained her dignity intact"
(p. 227). In spite of Dirk's earlier censure, Jacob marries his childhood
sweetheart, a "silly, ignorant coloured girl" (p. 80), and lives a reason-
ably happy, prosperous life. But when the degenerate Francis marries
(to spite his family) a *sambo* girl whose father, to Dirk's alarm, is "a
coarse, crude nigger" (p. 365), the girl's parents are far from pleased.
As Edward van Groenwegel reports:

The truth of the matter is that Francis got her pregnant, and the parents
only agreed to her marrying Francis to prevent her living in a state of
sin. . . . The impression I gained was that they are even less happy
about the match than we are. (p. 366)

The news from England of the queen's awarding of a baronetcy to
Reginald Greenfield, the son of Graham and Rose, is felt by Dirk as
the final twist of the knife; for, had he not insisted on Graham's
changing his name, the family would have received some of the
reflected glory: "and to think that it might have been Sir Reginald
van Groenwegel. That hurt" (p. 452). Later he says, "Black blood. I
might have been richer in spirit had I taught myself not to scorn it"

(p. 489); and whereas Graham ". . . had conquered the warp in his nature, and had come through to peace of mind in the final decades of his life" (p. 495), Dirk takes refuge in a fatalistic philosophy of hereditary accident:

In the final reckoning each member of our family will achieve only that which his inborn nature dictates that he is capable of achieving. The strong will prove strong. The weak will prove weak. (p. 427)

This sounds suspiciously like the attempt of a disillusioned man to cheer himself up; and with his visions of van Groenwegel power and glory falling in ruins around him, his impassioned outburst—

"The sexual urge. *That* is the driving force, my child, behind all our actions and all our destinies. It colors our lives from birth to grave." (p. 498)

—far from being Mittelholzer's view of a world in which sexual anarchy prevails, is an expression of Dirk's failure to "conquer the warp in his nature" and to achieve a *balance* of physical and moral strength. The real driving force, heredity, which, in Mittelholzer's view, could provide the potential both for success and failure in achieving this balance, is shown to be the only influence over which one can have absolutely no control: the unpredictable force which constantly mocks the arrogance of "whoremaster man" and makes nonsense of his pretensions. It is Hubertus's wider, more humane vision that finally provides a counterbalance to the van Groenwegel obsession with "blood":

I believe in the brotherhood of men on earth—not in the brotherhood of separate nations. . . . My loyalty has always been to human kind—not to a nation. (*Hubertus*, 1954, p. 226)

Any obsessive, narrow view of loyalty, Mittelholzer seems to be suggesting (such as the view of a Hendrickje or a Dirk), inevitably involves self-delusion. The novel—and the trilogy—ends as old Patrick Baxter-Hough (a "white" descendant of the van Groenwegels), taking an after-dinner stroll along a Georgetown street in 1953, pauses to amuse himself by listening to a political address. He instantly dislikes the political complexion of the young East Indian speaker: "Confounded fool," he mutters as he passes on, "thank God he's no relative of mine!" (p. 515). This is Mittelholzer's final, wry comment: for

"Georgie Boodoo" is also a bearer of van Groenwegel blood, and Patrick's casual dismissal of the "coffee-complexioned man" (p. 515)—an attitude all too common in the well-off, "respectable," "local-white" upper class of the colony, at the time—is itself ironic; for the socialist, multi-racial party the man represents—the People's Progressive Party—did, in fact, come to power in 1953 and provided the first impulse for what was later to become the Co-operative Republic of Guyana.

The progress through the trilogy of the ancestral "blood" of the van Groenwegels reflects Mittelholzer's enduring preoccupation with "two-ness" and the need for psychic integration. The pattern which evolves may be summarized as follows: an inherited strain of "bad blood" produces an inner division (strong/weak, spiritual/sensual) which, if unchecked, leads to degeneracy and the death-wish; but, if resisted, it can be channeled and redirected to good ends. The novels' historical framework serves mainly as a vehicle for the author's real concern with what is, in effect, a personal and psychological *malaise*; and Mittelholzer projects on to the events of the Guyanese past, with its burden of violence and sexual guilt, his own sense of an inner conflict of allegiances. Part African slave, part white slave-owner, Mittelholzer deliberately fragments his personality, as it were, allowing these two conflicting elements of his psyche to act out their opposition to each other in terms of Strength *versus* Weakness or, in Hubertus's case, Spirit *versus* Flesh. It is precisely because Mittelholzer is himself involved in this way that the novels' "moral purpose" appears to be undermined by intractable, contradictory impulses. But, as a closer reading of the novels' ironic purpose reveals, the author is aware of this conflict of opposites: in fact this is his main concern and gives a centrifugal unity to the work, for these irrevocably opposed forces are the expression of an indivisible whole, and, representing two facets of the author's personality, they are inevitably bound up together within the writing. In *Kaywana Blood* (1958), when Adrian van Groenwegel, Dirk's son, plays his own piano composition, his description of the piece reveals it as a musical allegory which summarizes the dualistic theme of the trilogy itself and reveals the author's deliberate, contrapuntal approach:

"It's loose in form," said Adrian, "but there are two twin themes, the one sad, the other gay. One is symbolic of the strong and the other of the weak, and they keep intermingling and—and warring with each other . . . and eventually the strong one takes command near the middle of the piece, and the other one seems as if it's going to die away, but suddenly it comes back into its own, and another warring takes place. Then towards the end you hear them both interlaced, and both are being resolved in a *perdendosi.*" (p. 454)

It is remarkable how closely Mittelholzer's embodiment, in the Kaywana novels, of a conflict between "strong" and "weak" elements reflects modern psychological views on the importance of patriarchal and matriarchal principles in society. According to Erich Fromm (invoking Bachofen's theory of "The Maternal Law"),[43] since "the principle of matriarchy is that of universality, while the patriarchal system is that of restrictions," [44] a blending of both is needed for a full and "sane" life, because

if they are opposed to each other, the matriarchal principle manifests itself in motherly over-indulgence and infantilization of the child, preventing its full maturity; fatherly authority becomes harsh domination and control, based on the child's fear and feelings of guilt.[45]

In other words, a situation develops in which the natural quality of each principle becomes exaggerated or perverted and a radical opposition between "strength" and "weakness" ensues. Any excessive bias toward either principle is equally undesirable, for

a viable and progressive solution lies only in a new synthesis of the opposites, one in which the opposition between mercy and justice is replaced by a union of the two on a higher level.[46]

Mittelholzer's "two twin themes," therefore, like his characterizations of Dirk and Graham van Groenwegel as "strong" and "weak," constitute an artistic rendering (whether conscious or unconscious) of this psychological theory: that a balanced union of the strong/male and weak/female principles alone can bring about psychic and social health. Mittelholzer's own awareness of inner conflict between the "male" and "female" aspects of his personality, "*Greensleeves*" weaving through the Sword motiv from *The Ring*," [47] would certainly seem to have provided the background to his lasting obsession with "strength" and "weakness." And in his characterization in presenting, for example, Hendrickje as a "phallic," power-seeking female, Graham as an excessively "soft" or "matriarchal" male, and Dirk as overly "masculine" and "hard," Mittelholzer has, with some insight, suggested both the symptoms and the inevitable result of a perversion of the patriarchal or matriarchal principles and revealed his overriding concern with psychic balance.

In *Sylvia* (1953) Mittelholzer retraced, to a large extent, the terrain of his own boyhood and young manhood, and, in the figure of Milton Copps, is himself present to comment on the narrow, coercive society whose strictures he so deeply resented. But in the Kaywana trilogy, though still personally involved through historical and family ties, he is at a sufficient distance from his subject—Guyana's colonial slave-history—to maintain a certain objectivity in the treatment of character and theme. He is able, therefore, to resist (in at least two of the novels of the trilogy) the tendency to identify with his characters, a tendency which, in most of his work, precludes a balanced view of the theory of "strength" and "weakness."

When one considers that the West Indian preoccupation with identity, with a psychological and cultural split (the most persistent theme in West Indian writing), has its origin in colonization and slavery, then the remarkable nature of Mittelholzer's sustained creative effort in the Kaywana trilogy, the act of bodying forth this psychological and cultural schism within the historical framework that gave it birth, becomes clear. For the conflict in the trilogy between "strength" and "weakness" is also the conflict between white and black, master and slave—the basis of that forlorn, sterile round of protest which, in erecting static biases of color or class, forces the West Indian to confront the "white" world in an attempt at self-identification. This, one suspects, is what lies behind Denis Williams's remark that, though not the greatest Guyanese work ever written, the trilogy was

. . . the one which *had* to be written . . . not only for clothing the bare bones of history with the vestments of the creative imagination, but also for proposing this unique problem of our relationship to the ancestor.[48]

The Kaywana trilogy is an epic, imaginative record of the peculiar social and historical reality of Guyana, a national novel, but it is also a prodigious, pioneering attempt to examine the cultural and emotional ambivalence which is a heritage of the West Indian past. By embodying the conflicting claims of history and heredity within the violent, ambiguous fortunes of the van Groenwegel family, Mittelholzer, like Nathaniel Hawthorne, attempted to exorcise the

ghosts of the past, and at the conclusion of the Kaywana trilogy might
almost be saying, with Hawthorne:

Let us thank God for having given us such ancestors; and let each successive generation thank Him, not less fervently, for being one step further
from them in the march of ages. ("Main Street," from *Twice-Told Tales*,
second series. London: Frederick Warne & Co., 1893, p. 70)

Hawthorne's ironic puppet-show, in which the New England "heritage" is seen to be ambiguous, has a great deal in common with
Mittelholzer's Kaywana trilogy: and the puppeteer's remarks remind
us of Hubertus van Groenwegel's ambivalent regard for the family
name, an attitude which lies at the heart of the Kaywana novels.
Divided within himself, Mittelholzer sought in his work both to examine and to identify this "two-ness." As a result, he is generally, to
an extraordinary degree, emotionally involved in his fiction, so that it
is never safe, in reading his work, to accept a superficial estimate
(even if it appears to be Mittelholzer's own) of events or characters.
The real problems of any critical exegesis of his novels come from the
fact that deeper levels of meaning are often overlaid by self-conscious
or prolix writing, and trivial incident and superficial characterization
often coincide with real insights. It is therefore possible to discover
within the novels as a whole both a Tragic Vision and the frivolous
"free-ranging fantasies" of a "moralist manqué." If there is a tragic
element which rescues Mittelholzer's work from the category of the
merely trivial, then it is to be found in the Faustian theme that underscores so much of his writing: the split in consciousness which, unless
repaired through an associative effort—an "at-onement" of Spirit and
Flesh, Strength and Weakness, leads to repression and the consequent
death-wish.

CHAPTER 2

Background to Exile

I *George Lamming (b. 1927)*

IN West Indian literature one sees these two kinds of division again and again. Indeed, the development of the writers' work is often powered by his own reactions to these inner, conflicting forces.

In George Lamming's partly autobiographical *In the Castle of My Skin* (1953), young G feels himself to be part of the communal village experience; he and his friends are close to the land and the "folk." But as the boy grows up he discovers himself to be more and more an individual, a stranger in his own society. His gradual alienation from friends, from the village, and finally from the island environment is more than a case of "growing up," of leaving the world of childhood behind. And it is not finally a question of class nor even of education, but of sensibility. For G has the questing, sensitive awareness of the creative artist. And in his development the natural, undifferentiated world of the village and the world of literature and art inevitably draw apart. The gulf looms, even where (as in Mais's case) there is no irresistible cultural pull toward Europe. G's overriding concern becomes the need to *preserve* this new identity, his integrity as a private individual, "the you that's hidden somewhere in the castle of your skin." It is a self-protective measure in a society that apparently can no longer contain or nourish the individual mind. Near the end of the book, G, a high-school product by now, cannot find acceptance with the villagers, nor can he relate meaningfully to his new status:

If I asserted myself they made it clear that I didn't belong just as Bob, Trumper and Boy Blue later insisted that I was no longer one of the boys. Whether or not they wanted to they excluded me from their world just as my memory of them and the village excluded me from the world of the High School. (p. 220)

Yet G, at the end of the book, recognizes that the reason for his sense of alienation is not simply the high school. Finally, he says,

"When I review these relationships they seem so odd. I have always been here on this side and the other person there on that side, and we have both tried to make the sides appear similar in needs, desires and ambitions. But it wasn't true. It was never true." (p. 261)

Emigration, exile, is the obvious next step. But in the next novel, *The Emigrants* (1954), there is another disillusionment and the inevitable return, the subject of *Of Age and Innocence* (1958) and, in particular, *Season of Adventure* (1960), which embodies an act of repossession of the native landscape, a reorientation of feeling through the experience of Fola in the *tonelle* during the ceremony of souls. But San Cristobal is an imaginary island, where the Haitian vodun ceremony can effect a "return to roots" alongside the music of the steel band as a measure of the society's indigenous cultural health. Even if one accepts, through Fola's "conversion," the cultural return to the "folk," one is left with that other dilemma: that of the artist, Chiki, who feels that his creative talent is drying up. Caught between his peasant origins—the world of the *tonelle*—and his European-oriented Christian education, he cries because he is afraid that his creative growth is stunted.

Chiki will not paint again because he thinks he is a man imprisoned in his paradox for all time: the paradox of what he is and what he cannot do. (p. 366)

This is a persistent symptom of a psychological and cultural division which still needs to be exorcised. Indeed, in *The Pleasures of Exile* (1960) Lamming explicitly sought exile to *confront* that other culture, the world of Prospero, in an attempt at self-definition. This was a head-on, articulate tackling of that deeper, cultural schizophrenia. For Lamming it is important that Caliban and Prospero should meet again within a new horizon,

. . . for it is only when they work together in the context of that horizon that the psychological legacy of their original contract will have been annulled. (*Pleasures of Exile*, p. 159)

Only then, when the ghosts of the past have been laid, can "each return to the skin without any inhibitions imposed by the exterior attributes of the Castle" (p. 159).

The problem, however, turned out to be more complicated. The characters were not as clear-cut anymore; the scene had altered and the framework of *The Tempest* proved too neat, too classical to fit the modern reality of such a confrontation. And now Caliban too had suffered a sea-change. He discovers that "Albion too was once a colony like ours":[1]

For it is that mutual experience of separation from their original ground which makes both master and slave colonial. To be colonial is to be in a state of exile. (*Pleasures of Exile,* p. 229)

And so the return journey begins in *The Pleasures of Exile,* leading directly to *Season of Adventure* in the newly independent republic of San Cristobal. But the novel ends with the fall of the First Republic, the silencing of the steel bands, Chiki's sense of being in limbo, a state of emergency. Powell, man of the people, has turned murderer, and the split between the "folk" and the educated artist/elite asserts itself. As Lamming writes in his "author's note," education had

earned me a privilege which now shut Powell [his half brother: his "other half"] and the whole *tonelle* right out of my future. (p. 332)

We are back with the central dilemma of G in the castle of his skin. And, ironically, it is the unlovable president of San Cristobal, Dr. Kofi James-Williams Baako, an academic, who has virtually the last sobering word:

. . . The main problem was language. It was language which caused the First Republic to fall. And the Second would suffer the same fate; the Second and the Third, unless they tried to find a language which was no less immediate than the language of the drums. (p. 363)

After a silence of eleven years, Lamming published *Water with Berries* (1971). It is, as he said in an interview, "my old Prospero/Caliban theme. . . . The story is built around the fortunes of three young artists, Caribbean artists in exile" (p. 18).[2] For Caliban's soul still frets (like that of Stephen Dedalus in Joyce's *A Portrait of the Artist as a Young Man,* 1916) in the shadow of Prospero's language, and another confrontation becomes necessary, since, as Lamming eloquently explains:

Caliban received not just words, but language as symbolic interpretation, as instrument of the exploring consciousness. . . . The future of his development, however independent, . . . would always be in some way inextricably tied up with that pioneering aspect of Prospero. Caliban . . . would have to find a way of breaking that contract, which got sealed by *language*, in order to restructure some alternative reality for himself.[3]

But this is the main theme of the essays in *The Pleasures of Exile*. This return to confront Prospero is therefore a more concerted attack. The artist Teeton (another, older version of Chiki, of *Season of Adventure*) and his friends Derek, the actor, and Roger, the East Indian musician concerned about caste and the dangers of taint, are now all aspects of Caliban. And their motive is revolutionary violence. Prospero's domain is a reality they must smash so as to reach a point of psychic reality within themselves. Again Lamming's own comment vis-à-vis Fanon's views on revolutionary violence is illuminating:

. . . Violence may be necessary as an exorcising instrument. Even if, in fact, a victory could be won without violence, the demons would remain.[4]

The Old Dowager, Teeton's kindly landlady, has to stand in for Prospero and Teeton murders her, coldly, as a therapeutic, emotional necessity. Prospero is no longer available, and there has to be a killing, so the Old Lady must die. Their need for revenge, however, is not so easily exorcised. And these revolutionaries cannot now turn back. There will be no return voyage home. Reality itself has altered, and the world of the black man in England is their New Reality.

Lamming's most recent novel, *Natives of My Person* (U.S., 1972), is an exceedingly complex work, full of allegorical and historical meanings and echoes. It is an embodiment of all his themes: a kind of reviewing process in which he appears to take stock of things. Not for nothing is the ship to which all the characters are bound as to each other called the *Reconnaissance*. The book is divided into three parts: "Breaking Loose," where a symbolic voyage to San Cristobal is undertaken (the storm they encounter reminds us of *The Tempest* theme); the section called "The Middle Passage"; and finally "The Women." What is fascinating about the Commandant, officers, and crew of this symbolic ship (Donne and his crew in Harris's *Palace of*

the Peacock come to mind here) is the remarkable way in which they
are dependent, each in a special sense, on the whole organization of
their floating castle, a community which exists on two levels of time—
the late sixteenth/early seventeenth century and the present.

The Commandant is a sea-changed Prospero who sets out to do
more than rule. He now feels a creative need to break with his own
world, to help found another, more valid society. Each of the characters seems to have a personal dilemma to solve. Particularly interesting is the character Pinteados, the stranger from another continent
who is the ship's pilot. He is a foreigner, disliked, but vital for the
community's survival. The note of tolerance is new. As Lamming
puts it, referring to the role of Pinteados:

This is like modern situations, where the technical agents in what are
called developing societies are usually foreigners. . . . He depicts . . .
the indispensability of the technical man in any operation.[5]

Another development is the suggestion in the section "The Middle
Passage," that *both* black slave and white master suffered a "middle
passage," the whites going through a period of spiritual brutality in
their own lives, a kind of inner penalty for their outer actions of rap-
ine and plunder. But there are no social or political solutions offered.
The all-powerful House of Trade which owns and administers the
ships renders the independence of the *Reconnaissance* null and void.
The analogy is with the huge international corporations—Big
Business—which so often underwrite the "independence" of developing countries.

But there is, in the women who have arrived at Black Rock by a
separate boat, a hint at a possible reorientation of society. The future
rests with them—with a new relationship between them and their
men. This too is a new note in Lamming's work. The reclamation of a
whole society through a more balanced—less patriarchal—relationship between the sexes, rather than by political revenge. Of course
the alienated artist is still there, represented by the character Ivan, a
painter. But his dilemma, of having creative vision but lacking direct
communication with the masses, is accepted without fuss, as a condition attaching by definition to the creative imagination.

What is striking, in the development of Lamming's work, is the
way in which the "castle of his skin" is expanded and extended to
include more and more contradictory elements of experience as "natives of his person." But this is just another way of saying that the

writer's primary concern is with the range and quality of his experience of life. Only when the creative writer or artist has allowed himself to become *vulnerable to experience*, when he has "earned his exile," can he begin to weld together the two halves of his social and
cultural fracture, to accept the fact of his alienation in spite of the
force of his commitment.

II V. S. Naipaul (b. 1932)

The nature and quality of *any* writer's work is, of course, inextricably bound up with his social and cultural attitudes. Under pressure of
a limited racial, cultural, or political outlook, one's actual experience
of the world is, inevitably, blinkered. For the Caribbean writer, however, caught between the competing claims of a European and a
"Third World" sensibility, between the dominant values of an Old
World and the cultural realities of a New, the twin dangers of schizophrenia and mimicry are particularly insidious. For the Caribbean
person one form of cultural mimicry can all too easily lead to another. The insistence, however eloquent or dramatic, on an "identity" often disguises a subtle wish for dependence, for an unearned,
automatic respect. As Derek Walcott puts it,

Once we have lost our wish to be white, we develop a longing to become
black. And these two may be different, but they are still careers. (Preface
to *Dream on Monkey Mountain and Other Plays*. London: Jonathan Cape,
1962, p. 20)

This is the cultural and racial schizophrenia, first noticeable in the
work of Edgar Mittelholzer, which runs like a *leitmotiv* through the
literature of the Caribbean. One commentator[6] argues that the special urgency of the literature springs from the "European factor"
within, and suggests that Naipaul is a "curious casualty" of this factor
"with restricted possibilities of further contribution, not technically,
but philosophically, to West Indian literature." And one remembers
Lamming's bitter attack on Naipaul for his lack of "peasant feeling"
and for the "castrated satire" of his work. But Naipaul's sense of
alienation grew out of the same kind of situation experienced, in a
different way, perhaps, by Lamming. The young narrator of *Miguel
Street*, like the young boy G of Lamming's *In the Castle of My Skin*,
is educated away from the life of his poor community. But this split
between the people of the village or street and himself is largely the

measure of a gap in sensibility. The sensitive awareness of the boy sees through and beyond the social life, the apparent wholeness of his community, to the essential loneliness and despair of its individual members, who are (whether they know it or not) in a state of exile. This is the meaning in *Miguel Street* of the episode of Black Wordsworth. The poet's very individuality makes him an eccentric, an outsider within his own society, where he is condemned to remain artistically stunted: a mimic-poet, a *black* Wordsworth. Naipaul, one feels, wished to leave the Caribbean to avoid the frustration of talent mirrored in the lonely death of Black Wordsworth. It is this fear that one confronts initially in the work of both Mittelholzer and Naipaul, a fear of being trapped by one's origins. It is no coincidence that they share the Nightmare of Return: in *The Middle Passage* (1962) V. S. Naipaul's nightmare—

. . . For many years afterwards in England, falling asleep in bed-sitters with the electric fire on, I had been awakened by the nightmare that I was back in tropical Trinidad. (p. 41)

—is, as we have seen, similar to Mittelholzer's, recorded in *With a Carib Eye* (1958).

. . . And then, with a shudder, I would awake to find myself in Bagshot, Surrey or in Montreal, Canada or on the Maxwell Coast of Barbados, and the relief would be tremendous. (pp. 134–35)

The Middle Passage (1960) is Naipaul's confrontation with this nightmare, and its partial exorcism. For part of the fear lay in the sense of cultural isolation from a larger, Metropolitan concept of "the best that has been thought and said," a culture of which colonial Trinidad seemed a poor reflection. Such a view, just or unjust, coupled with an almost ascetic honesty and respect for the truth of a situation, made exile, for Naipaul, a personal necessity:

You have to become adept in looking for the truth of your own responses. I think it's much more important for me, coming from a place which is not real, a place which is imperfectly made, and a place where people are, really, quite inferior, because they demand so little of themselves. They are colonials, in a type of perpetual colonial situation. Coming from such a society, I didn't really have views of my own. I didn't know what I thought about anything, because the world was out of my hands. . . . In writing my first four or five books (including books which perhaps people think of as my big books) I was simply *recording my reactions* to the world; I hadn't come to any conclusion about it. . . . Since then, I have begun to analyse. First of all, the deficiencies of the society from which I came; and then, through that, what goes to make this much more complex society in which I have worked so long.[7]

At least two important issues emerge from that provocative statement. The writer's commitment, not to his "imperfect" society with its "inferior" inhabitants, but to the "truth of his own responses," urges the retort "So why didn't you try with your superior gifts, to help to *enrich* the poor soil that, after all, produced you?" But this would be to underestimate the thoroughness of the colonial process itself. To write or speak honestly about one's own undeveloped society is a hazardous enough undertaking, but to have attempted it in a *colonial*, undeveloped society would have been to invite ridicule, scorn, and disbelief (as Roger Mais and Edgar Mittelholzer discovered). A commitment to truth has always been a guarantee of alienation.

The second issue raised by Naipaul's remarks concerns the approach to his fiction, the fact that his first four or five books—which would include *The Mystic Masseur* (1957), *The Suffrage of Elvira* (1958), *Miguel Street* (1959), *A House for Mr. Biswas* (1961), and *The Middle Passage* (1962)—were written from a need to *record* his reactions, rather than to analyze or understand them: The "castrated satire" that Lamming finds in Naipaul's early work (his remark was made in 1960) in the devastating ironic humor especially of *The Mystic Masseur* and *The Suffrage of Elvira* has its origin, then, in this urgency to record a sense of personal rootlessness, of panic, of alienation. In the same interview Naipaul explains:

At first I looked for this release in humour, but as the horizon of my writing expanded I sought to reconstruct my disintegrated society, to impose order on the world, to seek patterns. . . . I had to find that degree of intellectual comfort, or I would have gone mad.[8]

This element of rootlessness and personal disintegration was already present in the writing of *Miguel Street*, in an unusually tender, almost tragic story about the death of the boy's father—which Naipaul decided to omit from the book. This is "The Enemy," a short episode which was published later as part of the collection *A Flag on the Island* (1967). Briefly, the "enemy" in the story is the boy's mother. An

only child, he early gains his mother's disapproval because of his
tendency, like his father, to be an individual in a society where individualism is regarded as undesirable and antisocial. After a quarrel,
his parents separate and the boy chooses to stay with his artistic, eccentric father. They draw closer together and the boy learns (as he
does from Black Wordsworth in *Miguel Street*) the wonder and value
of the world of art and intellect. The father dies during a thunderstorm—a traumatic experience for the boy—and his mother, "the
enemy," reclaims him. A cut above the average, the boy gets "12
marks out of 10" for an essay, and when his mother finally believes
him, she invites him to sit near her. The conflict which develops is a
prefiguring of the grown man's dilemma: the gifted individual's refusal to conform to an undifferentiated society's demands, and his simultaneous need for the comfort it offers:

It had become a struggle between two wills. I was prepared to drown
rather than dishonour myself by obeying. . . . She belted me soundly,
and my nose bled, but still I didn't sit in the hammock. . . . So she remained the enemy. She was someone from whom I was going to escape as
soon as I was big enough. That was, in fact, the main lure of adulthood.
(p. 71)

A House for Mr. Biswas has been described as a classic struggle for
personality against a society that denies it, and it is significant that
the story of "The Enemy," in an extended form, is placed at the structural center of this novel. It is a turning point for Mr. Biswas. His
failure to "paddle his own canoe," to live on his own in the Green
Vale house—the first house he builds—is a failure of premature individuation. He is still too self-divided to cut himself off from the faceless mass of Tulsidom. Recuperating in the Blue Room, he realizes an
important truth: individuality is a hazardous possession whose other
aspect is isolation:

Hanuman House was an organism that possessed a life, strength and
power to comfort which was quite separate from the individuals who com-
posed it. (p. 302, my italics)

Mr. Biswas's second house, at Shorthills, is also incomplete, a reflection of his still unformed personality:

The house was not painted. It stood red-raw in its unregulated green setting, not seeming to invite habitation so much as decay. (p. 424)

His attempt at a celebratory bonfire goes dangerously wrong, and the resultant bushfire creates a desolation for which Biswas stands accused, in spite of his comic attempt to salvage the situation:

Morning revealed the house, still red and raw, in a charred and smoking desolation. Villagers came running to see. . . .
"Charcoal, charcoal," Mr. Biswas called to them. "Anybody want charcoal?" . . . "Best thing for the land." . . . "Best sort of fertilizer." (p. 432)

He is, again mercifully, released from private ownership and moves back to the unpleasantness, but relative safety, of overcrowded, shared accommodation. And it is here, in Mrs. Tulsi's Port-of-Spain house, crammed in among W. C. Tuttle, Govind, and Chinta and the readers and learners, that Biswas ironically begins his rise from investigator of Deserving Destitutes to Community Welfare Officer.

Thrown out to make way for Owad, Mrs. Tulsi's pride and joy, Biswas nevertheless gains a significant victory. When Owad (whose Marxist socialism is merely a blind for his self-regarding snobbishness) leaves in a fit of rage, unable to stand the squabbling, the hitherto faceless, unfriendly Tulsi husband, Govind, comes to Biswas's room and tacitly acknowledges the respect he now feels:

"Mohun!" His voice was kind. Mr. Biswas was overwhelmed to tears. "Communism, like charity," he said to Govind, "should begin at home." "We know, we know," Govind said. (p. 557)

The house Mr. Biswas finally buys is still not his own. Heavily mortgaged, it turns out to be a very different house from the vision of a desirable home which he had seen in the rain:

The vines of the Morning Glory spattered with small red flowers. . . . The height of the house, the cream and grey walls, the white frames of doors and windows, the red brick sections with white pointing. (p. 563)

But even then, Biswas had instinctively realized that such a vision was impossible for him. "These things Mr. Biswas took in at once, and knew that the house was not for him" (p. 563).

But Biswas's effort to be accommodated, if not entirely successful, is certainly heroic, given the obstacles placed before him by a crab-barrel society and by his own lack of a personal center of gravity. For

Biswas's struggle for individuality is complicated by the process of cultural change, of creolization. And it is this disturbing process which underlies Biswas's sense of a disordered, crumbling world in which merely to have survived is to have succeeded.

In Mittelholzer's *Corentyne Thunder*, Baijan, aspiring to the middle-class social level of the Ramjits, has already left his peasant origins behind. For the Ramjits represent the almost creolized Hindu of the 1940s. Yet the peasant status and sensibilities of Ramgolall, Beena, and Kattree, though rooted in the land, nevertheless represent a stage in Hindu creolization: the result of immigration and indenture. India, for Ramgolall, is only a vague memory.

In *Biswas*, Tulsidom is still fairly close to an original Indian culture—as the carved figures and paintings of Hanuman the monkey-god and the facts and artifacts of the Tulsi household suggest. Hanuman House, founded by pundit Tulsi, a respected Hindu priest whose links with Mother India were still intact during his lifetime, is a recognizable—though decayed and often spurious—piece of Old India with "Ceylon" as their backyard. Hindi is spoken still, and it is English that is reserved for formal or exotic use. Tulsidom represents all the rigid traditional and ritualistic qualities of the separatist Hindu community of Trinidad—a bastion against creolization and individualism.

Biswas (like Baijan and Kattree), however, has come from a peasant, hut-dwelling atmosphere where family bonds have already been split up and degrees of precedence, like traditional, communal rituals, have lost most of their significance or appeal. The progress of industrialization has damaged even his peasant roots, his father's hut ploughed under, his navel-string's burial place lost. Biswas's creolization, in other words, has already progressed considerably. One has to add to this his experience of school life, his discovery of other more liberal modes of behavior, like Alec's or Lal's, or of the maverick Hindu Bhandat and his Chinese wife.

To Biswas, therefore, the community at Hanuman House presents a formidable, hierarchical structure—at first fascinating, even attractive (like Shama's shy smile) but later oppressive and stifling. To the as yet uncreolized, atavistic Tulsis, Biswas must naturally seem a rebel just as it is only natural that Biswas should rebel against the facelessness and monolithic conservatism of Tulsidom. An individual mind like Biswas's, however comic or eccentric, is an automatic threat to the conformity required by the Tulsi clan system. Criticizing, speaking Trinidadian Creole English instead of Hindi, Biswas undermines the Tulsi community at its weakest points, by exposing the inevitable signs and portents of its own growing creolization which, denied, leaves hypocrisy at the center of a stubborn Hinduism. The young "gods" wear crucifixes, and even Mrs. Tulsi has strong Catholic leanings, facts upon which Biswas pounces gleefully. He uses his own flair for words to ridicule the whole concept of Hanuman House, calling it the "monkey house," and finally the "zoo."

And it is liberal education that sounds the death knell of Tulsidom. When Owad returns, degreed and traveled, he is an egotistic snob in spite of his talk about communism. When he leaves the family begins to break up. But if Naipaul shows us the negative, repressive aspect of the Tulsi cultural machine, he also makes it clear that it is a *flawed* machine, and that the Tulsis have in fact lost the greater purpose and vision of their founder. The Shorthills adventure points up the inner poverty of spirit which the apparent solidity of Hanuman House conceals. For the scramble to make *personal* gain out of the new situation makes the adventure a sordid one. Private commercial incentive takes precedence (it had always underpinned the society at Arwacas) over the community's welfare. The Tulsis are condemned, not for their anachronistic conventionalism, but for their lack of moral integrity. They resist the movement toward creolization, but have no *genuine* cultural or ethical standards to defend. It is not, in short, Hinduism that is discredited, but the emptiness and show (like the facade of Hanuman House) that have replaced true Hinduism. "The virtue had gone out of the family," as Biswas observes. The protection Tulsidom offered was the protection of anonymity.

It is evidence, too, of Naipaul's tough-minded approach to the problem of creolization and the individual response that Biswas's progress is haphazard, accidental, and almost futile. Creolization has weaned him away from the engulfing Hindu matrix, but his personal equipment is shaky, his Brahminism tenacious, and his life becomes therefore a lonely struggle. Tulsidom may have many pains, but individualism can have few pleasures. In the continuing process of creolization, Biswas is very much a transitional figure. It is in Anand, one feels, that the process will continue and perhaps find resolution. It is not the concept of a faceless society that is distressing, but the inability to relate to it in a creative, meaningful way. If the Hindu community of the Tulsis is amorphous, imprisoning, denying the individual's need to be a separate entity or to have a personal, private dimension, then it is also true to say that Biswas lacks that genuine quality of balance, of emotional wholeness, which true individuality requires.

His efforts to be housed, to be *accommodated* as an individual, are therefore inevitably subject to failure.

Like Naipaul, Biswas, aware of his gift for language, his sensitive awareness of his world, but alienated from an imperfect society because of these things, seeks release in humor while he attempts, through literature, to reintegrate his divided self, to impose order on a fragmented world. One incident in the novel beautifully illustrates Biswas's awareness of an inner need for wholeness. He writes a poem, and "the poem written, his selfconsciousness violated, he was whole again" (p. 484). It is a poem about the death of his mother, the "enemy" whose love he had always needed. He reads the poem to a group of literary friends: it is the first genuine expression of his own, inner self:

"It is a poem" he said, "in prose." . . . Then he disgraced himself. Thinking himself free of what he had written, he ventured on his poem boldly, and even with a touch of self-mockery. But as he read, his hands began to shake, the paper rustled; and when he spoke of the journey his voice failed. It cracked and kept on cracking; his eyes tickled. But he went on, and his emotion was such that at the end no one said a word. (pp. 484–85)

Biswas, the outsider, never finds the order, the pattern that he seeks within his disintegrating society—one of the harshest ironies in the book is surely his government job as Community Welfare Officer—but his maimed attempts give him a heroic stature. There is a hint that, for his children, at least, life may be more coherent. But, as Biswas thinks about the future, the images that come to mind point not to the Caribbean, but to Europe:

In a northern land, in a time of new separations and yearnings, in a library grown suddenly dark, the hailstones beating against the windows, the marbled endpaper of a dusty, leatherbound book would disturb. . . . (p. 581)

And it is in Europe, in England, that Ralph Singh, failed husband, failed businessman, politician in exile, sits down, in an alien boardinghouse, symbol of his rootlessness and his crippled emotional life, to attempt to make order of a fragmented, meaningless existence. It is a coldly analytical exercise, an unnervingly accurate dissection. It is not merely a reaction to the world of his experience, but an attempt to discover a pattern, "to impose order on my own history" (p. 243), as Singh puts it. At the comparatively young age of forty, he is completely self-alienated, withdrawn from all society, resigned to "the final emptiness." This is the logical result of an excessive fear of loss of self, of one's private existence.

It is a fear that permeates Naipaul's work. In *An Area of Darkness* (1964), himself an Indian in an Indian crowd in Bombay, Naipaul can write:

It was like being denied part of my reality. . . . I was faceless. I might sink without a trace into that Indian crowd. (p. 43)

But no less obvious is his Brahminic fear of "taint," and the resultant respect for cultural pedigree which makes him admire the Aryan qualities which he sees in the Sikh who befriends him on a train:

The Sikhs puzzled and attracted me. They were among the few whole men in India, and of all Indians they seemed closest in many ways to the Indians of Trinidad. (p. 222)

It is this cultural elitism, rather than a specifically *European* factor, which produces in Naipaul an instinctive respect for "purity," pedigree, tradition. Even in his journalism there is this fastidiousness of reaction, a respect for the elitist, sybaritic quality in others. In an *Observer* Colour Supplement article (London, December 10, 1971) in an interview with the successful young British artist David Hockney, Naipaul describes Hockney as gentle, serene, *flawlessly* blond. (Not simply "blond": one notices again that Naipaulian respect for the "untainted".) And Hockney is presented as successful not only because his work is popular and fetches high prices, but also, more significantly, because the Bradford-born artist has escaped his unimaginative, narrow, working-class background; from his own "Miguel Street." In India, Naipaul's vision of the cave dwellers of Kashmir as "handsome, sharp-featured men, descendants, I felt, of Central Asian horsemen" (*An Area of Darkness*, p. 129), reappears in *The Mimic Men* (1967) as the hero's vision of a magnificent past heritage, now lost. Naipaul's disillusionment with India is in direct proportion to his longing for an "unsullied" cultural heritage; his reaction to the Indians' apparently casual attitude to defecation is therefore almost frenzied:

Indians defecate everywhere . . . beside railway tracks . . . on the beaches; they defecate on the hills . . . on the streets. . . . These squatting figures are never spoken of . . . never written about; they are not mentioned in novels or stories; they do not appear in feature films or documentaries. . . . But the truth is that *Indians do not see these squatters.* (p. 70)

One is reminded of a similar personal alarm, parodied in a poem by Jonathan Swift, an ironist and satirist with whom Naipaul has occasionally been compared. In Swift's "tragical elegy," *Cassinus and Peter* (1731), the romantic lover, Cassinus, is dejected, his emotional life in ruins because of a dreadful discovery he has made about his beloved, the fair and beautiful Caelia. His friend Peter drags the awful secret to light. Cassinus laments:

> How would her virgin soul bemoan
> A crime to all her sex unknown!
> . . . And yet I dare confide in you
> So take my secret and adieu!
> Nor wonder how I lost my wits
> Oh! Caelia, Caelia, Caelia shits.

"And a very good thing, too," as D. H. Lawrence observed, "or the poor girl would really have had a serious problem." In *The Mimic Men* one witnesses the withdrawal of the hero's fastidious ego in an attempt to preserve identity against "taint," against external, disintegrative forces. Singh, adrift between the Caribbean and Europe, the New World and the Old, becomes obsessed with self-preservation:

. . . It became urgent now for me. Before it had been part of fantasy, part of the urge to . . . return to lands I had fashioned in my imagination, lands of horsemen, high plains, mountains and snow. . . . Now I felt only the need to get away. (p. 145)

Unable to see the Caribbean as anything more than a rubbish heap of broken cultures, Singh turns more and more toward the Old World, seeking a filial relationship with a host culture that promises "wholeness," or as a last resort, anonymity. In this respect, his relationship with the English girl, Sandra, is instructive. Sandra herself is a composite sex and mother figure, providing both sensuality and security. But for Singh, even the sensuality relates to his need for dependency on a parent figure. The description of this European mother figure is worth quoting in some detail:

Her looks were of the sort that improves with the strength and definition of maturity. She was tall; her bony face was longish and I liked the suggestion of thrust in her chin and lower lip. . . . And there was a coarseness about her skin which enchanted me. . . . There was firmness and precision in her movements. . . . Not even the macintosh could hide the fullness of her breasts, to which I had for some little time been admitted. They were not the self-supporting cut apples of the austere French ideal; but breasts curving and rounded with a weight just threatening pendent excess, which the viewer, recognizing the inadequacy and indeed the crudity of the cupping gesture, instinctively stretches out a hand to support . . . breasts which in the end madden the viewer because, faced with such completeness of beauty, he does not know what to do. (p. 43)

That insistence on the *aesthetic* nature of Sandra's physical beauty is a red herring. The real attraction for Singh are those pendent, sustaining breasts "to which [he] had for some little time been admitted": Sandra as ruling matriarch. And, of course, the sense of protection which, as a representative of the host-culture, she offers. When she practically orders him to propose, Singh accepts abjectly. Lovemaking in the novel is a clinical, detached affair: "Two private bodies on a stained bed." For it is not sex, but a filial attachment that Singh needs. Later in a flashback, Singh, a young boy about to experience his first sense of being on his own (he is to take part in the school sports), remembers a dream of the night before:

I had dreamt that I was a baby again and at my mother's breast. What joy! The breast on my cheek and mouth: a consoling weight, the closeness of soft, smooth flesh. . . . My mother rocked and I had the freedom of her breast. . . . What pain then, what shame, to awaken! (p. 116)

In fact, there is much to suggest that Singh remains emotionally dependent, at an oral, breast-oriented stage of development, unable to experience genuine love or meaningful sexual experience. His affair with young Lady Stella is described in terms of a childish sexual experiment. It is a play-relationship from which Singh can gain no emotional support or lasting pleasure. Stella's parting gift, *The House at Pooh Corner*, is an appropriate one: a reminder of Singh's immature, unfinished personality, like Biswas's, which is symbolized by the houses in the novel. The book begins with Singh's book-shaped room in Mr. Shylock's boardinghouse in London and ends in the dining room of a hotel where, seated behind a pillar, he can observe only the hands of another guest, also seated behind a pillar. In Isabella, as a child, he lived in his father's rickety house. On visits to his mother's family, who owned a solidly built house, he would jump on the floors, a precaution that made him feel safe before going to bed. Then there is Crippleville, which, ironically, is a success, but only in shallow, financial terms—a successful but shoddy piece of real estate. Later there is the ridiculously pretentious Roman house of Singh, the successful politician. Even the first house he and Sandra live in, in Isabella, is a synonym for rootlessness:

I had no feelings for the house as home, as personal creation. I had no things, no treasures, no collection even of books, no household gods, as Sandra would have said. (p. 71)

But for Naipaul's heroes (as for Mittelholzer's) the attempt to graft a fragmented self on to a European host-culture invariably ends in despair or tragedy. Asked in an interview if he could not

graft on to any main body, [Naipaul] said, wryly, turning down the corners of his mouth, that it was rather that the main bodies rejected the graft.[9]

And so Naipaul's success, like Biswas's, is only partial: the house is still mortgaged. The West Indian writer's "search for a place" still goes on. But it is from the journey itself, from the necessity of exile, that the literature, paradoxically, draws its strength. And, like all important journeys, it is a circular one: a journey of exile and return.

III   Garth St. Omer (b. 1924)

The trauma of exile and return is exemplified in the work of Garth St. Omer. Like Walcott, St. Omer is aware of the gulf between artistic or personal aspiration and an imprisoning island society, a gulf that grows wider on the writer's return. St. Omer's travelers, when they return, face a void. Walcott and St. Omer, St. Lucians, shared the same kind of background. The beauty of an island, rich in folklore with a unique folk language[10] accepted by all, rain forest and virginal, green mountains (where there are still people who have never seen a tourist): these things appear in Walcott's work and balance his despair. Garth St. Omer's vision, by contrast, is bleak, uncompromising. On a small, undeveloped, Catholic island, its main city ravaged by fire more than once, it must have been easy to develop a "precocious resignation to fate." St. Lucia's main cemetery (Catholic) is conspicuously situated alongside Vigie Airport, near the Castries city center: almost a deliberate reminder to those who come and go that death is the final destination. To earth we must all return. And it is this sense of bleak finality one finds in St. Omer's treatment of the theme of exile and return: a Homecoming to Fate.

In his novella, *Syrop* (1964), his first published work apart from short sketches and extracts in journals, the pattern of futility is already established. The edge of the fishing village, in a filthy shack by the sea, where Syrop, like Ti-Jean, the youngest of three children, lives with his blind father, is a swamp, a veritable cesspool. The eldest, Lescaut, a young man in his prime, is in jail for manslaughter; the daughter, Anne, is a vagrant and a whore. In this unpromising context there is to be a homecoming. Lescaut, whose estranged wife, incidentally, has now remarried, is about to be released after an eight-year sentence. The old, blind, and embittered father has disowned him as he has cursed and banished his daughter. Only young Syrop, who loves his brother, looks forward to this grim homecoming. In fact Syrop is the only figure of positive health in the story, the blind father's last hope for a better future. Though he is still, at fourteen, too young for the coming-of-age procession on the Catholic Feast of St. Peter and St. Paul (the patron saints of fishermen) he is lucky enough to qualify for the procession—regarded as a great privilege, a symbol of his entry to manhood. His brother's homecoming, ironically, is to be on the same day as the procession. The daughter, Anne, pregnant and in a vicious mood, visits and abuses the old man. During the fight between herself and Syrop (who tries to protect their father) the unborn fetus is fatally damaged. But worse is to come. Syrop, determined at least to get enough money to buy his brother a homecoming breakfast, joins the older boys in the harbor, diving for tourists' coins. He is unsuccessful and desperate, as the big liner begins to move out, and he prays silently that the sailor standing at the stern of the vessel, its propellers beginning to turn, will throw a coin. He is alone now in the water. The man tosses the coin, and Syrop, his prayer answered, dives and retrieves it. Unfortunately he is caught in the powerful undertow of the propellers, which drag him to his death. The coolness and the graphic, laconic style of this passage (characteristic of Garth St. Omer's work), give to Syrop's death a horrible, utterly fascinating quality of inevitability. Throughout the story, there is a compelling sense of the inevitability of death, and its almost total permeation of society. Syrop's headless, mangled body is laid out ritually on the wharf. The severed head is placed at the side of the body (an image which recurs in St. Omer's latest novel) while the crowd watches silently. Anne, bearing the now dead weight of her fetus, comes on the scene to denounce both the dead Syrop and the watchers of this grisly ritual. When the blind father is brought, he says quietly, "To die now, when you are still young, is a great privilege. You are a lucky boy" (p. 187). But the ritual is not complete until he touches the jagged, bloody stump of his son's neck and experiences the actual, sensuous shock which affirms the fact of death.

Syrop's death is presented as a necessary expiation of a whole society's guilt, the stain that is handed on from parent to child, from generation to generation like some malign disease. A legacy of futility. As Anne, his fallen daughter, tells the old man,

"I did what I did with the you in me. And if you detest me you have to detest yourself also. Because you are in me." (p. 160)

But, although St. Omer does not ever point to a moral or offer a solution, it is already clear in this first work, that the depressing fatalism and sterility of society are not only the result of a rooted poverty which depends on the tossed coin of the casual tourist, although both Walcott and St. Omer are aware of the damaging side effects: the essentially destructive undertow of tourism:

Hang out the flags, the assassins of culture come
wrapped in their hundred thousand dollar charm.
Whisk them all safely to the crisp hotel.
Flatter them all. . . .

Let the picturesque fisherman's picturesque poverty be
willing to row them to the historical cay
where Christopher kneeled, and with a witty remark
postpone the shark. . . .

Teach all the gulls to perform a white ballet,
to grin at cricketers on equality's field day.
Entice them with scarves, make the prize hen lay eggs,
Make a ballet Negres. . . .

Let the black hand at the tiller instruct the yachts
of the blonde's desire to avoid the spittled rocks.
Throw a coin nearer the propellers to see if the
    diver returns alive. . . .
("Montego Bay: Travelogue ii")

That is an extract from an early unpublished poem by Derek Walcott. The link with the death of Syrop is interesting. Certainly the gray world of *Syrop*, like that of Walcott's fishermen in *The Sea at Dauphin*, is one of unrelieved and bitter frustration, where death, "la mort," is more a blessing than a curse. It is the world, too, of an early twenty-minute radio play, written by Walcott in 1950 and called *Harry Dernier*. The name is a pun. "Dernier" is French for "last" and the hero is the last man in a world destroyed in some nuclear cataclysm. He is a castaway in an enormous, sterile desert: "Who am I? Who daren't explore/the fringes of my hand? The horizon has become/a boundary of bones." His is a monologue on loneliness and death. Some of the imagery of the play reappears in *The Castaway* (1965).

Garth St. Omer's novels center around this sargasso-like condition of existence from which escape, exile, is a logical step, and to which return is an act of courage leading to masquerade, madness, suicide. But, if the root of this original condition of depression and fatalism is not simply a matter of the sheer brute weight of society's poverty, where does the problem originate? Robert Lee, a young St. Lucian poet, has, in a dissertation on "The Themes in the Novels of Garth St. Omer" (April 1973, U.W.I., Cave Hill), located the roots of this problem of frustration and pessimism in the Catholic-based colonial framework of St. Lucian society. The characters in the novels are caught, as he puts it, "within the 'triangular barriers' of sin, guilt and punishment." Certainly, in *Syrop*, both Anne, the prostitute, and Lescaut, the criminal, are sinners whose guilt is punished not only by the law (in Lescaut's case) and by character and circumstance (Anne's pregnancy and possible death from fetal poisoning), but by their own father and the society which expects and exacts such a payment. Even the death of Syrop is not entirely blameless, merely an expiation of Evil by the death of Innocence. For Syrop is responsible for the death of Anne's baby. His prayer to God for the tossed coin is granted, but a terrible price is exacted for his "sin" against an unborn life. When the old, blind father suggests that he may have failed his children by not making them more religious, his nephew, Ti-son, instead of simply acknowledging this feeble attempt to accept blame, places the burden of guilt more squarely on the old man's shoulders:

"You gave them no bad example but you gave them no specific good ones either . . . you taught them to fear God . . . not to trust him." (p. 162)

It is this righteous negative attitude, the insistence on guilt and expiation, which underlies the society's view of itself, and erects a trinity of sin, guilt, and punishment as the framework of life. Paul Breville, in *J-, Black Bam and the Masqueraders* (1972), St. Omer's most recent novel, understands, at last, why his act of independence, his refusal to be forced into a loveless marriage, makes him an outcast unable, though well qualified, to get more than a menial job:

I saw that the whole town accepted the idea of sin, guilt and punishment. And that the church, before it forgave, always punished first. (p. 97)

It is then that he begins to appreciate the influence of "that squat, ugly edifice that crouched in the middle of the town" (p. 97). He is referring to the cathedral in Columbus Square, Castries.

But the Church in the colonial Caribbean not only legislated for fixed moral attitudes, it also reinforced Europe-based cultural norms. Beneficent or vengeful, the God one prayed to was white, remote, and foreign. His dark worshipers approached (as they did his religious and secular emissaries) with a double humility, as black sinners in a religious landscape whose dominant tone was white. So we are back, by another route, to the cultural and emotional split, the self-division which can fix a society in attitudes of hopelessness, despair, and resignation to fate, a resignation that is present even in the hero's apparent defiance in Walcott's play, *The Sea at Dauphin* (1954):

God is a White Man. The sky is his blue eye. His spit on Dauphin people is the sea. Don't ask me why a man must work so hard to eat for worm to get more fat. . . . You never curse God. I curse him and cannot die until His time.

It is, of course, true that his Catholic background is a central force in St. Omer's novels. The sin-guilt-punishment syndrome operates throughout the work and, though St. Omer does not preach, as Lee puts it, "His tone is that of the confessional. . . ." In *Room on the Hill* (1968), as in all the novels, this air of the confessional pervades. It achieves its greatest heights in *J-, Black Bam and the Masqueraders*, where chapters headed "Paul" are confessions of one brother (p. 5). There are also, of course, the Catholic Brothers who often appear in his work: successful as well as failed priests. One of the white characters—the headmaster—in Part Two of *Shades of Grey* (1968) is described as "a picture of colonial seediness," reminding Derek, the hero, of "Graham Greene's novels of expatriates in Africa and America" (p. 222). The analogy is apt, especially if one thinks of the whiskey priest of *The Power and the Glory* (1959), or of Scobie in *The Heart of the Matter* (1948). In Greene's Catholic universe, sin, guilt, and punishment become almost an obsession, while death is a blessed release.

Within this framework, the theme of personal sin and public expiation (giving, as it were, a religious twist to the conflict between private sensibility and public function), St. Omer's characters are very tightly linked. In fact, characters in early books reappear (often in greater depth) in the later ones. We first meet Derek Charles, briefly, in *A Room on the Hill*. In Part Two of *Shades of Grey* he is the main character. In Part One of the same book, Dr. Peter Breville and his wife, Phyllis, and their violently unhappy marriage are mentioned peripherally. In *Nor Any Country* (1969) their relationship and Peter's sense of despair, of panic on his return to the island, are the central elements. His relationship with his brother, Paul, who— "trapped" on the island—is becoming mentally unbalanced, is introduced. In *J-, Black Bam and the Masqueraders* (1972) the relationship between Peter and Paul is central, and Paul's voice, his own point of view, is more insistent. It is as if St. Omer is considering a particular group of characters, indeed a particular relationship between the homecoming intellectual and his less fortunate, trapped brethren in greater and greater depth. From a general, almost aerial survey of a society caught in the colonial mesh of poverty, guilt, and self-contempt (the world of *Syrop*) St. Omer focuses, in successive novels, on the nature of the educated individual's relationship to his society and (with *J-, Black Bam and the Masqueraders*) on the divided intellectual's relationship with friend, brother, and, finally, with himself. Exile, escape from a restricting, uncreative society leads to the inevitable Return. But, if in St. Omer's work exile is seen primarily as a need to break out of the psychological prison of guilt and self-contempt, then the Return—at its deepest level—suggests the equally vital need to live with the confusion and pain and frustration that a genuine at-one-ment involves.

Garth St. Omer's work starts from a consideration of the rootless, colonial society's frustration and resignation to fate and develops this theme, relating it to the individual's need for personal stability as a necessary prelude to any meaningful dialogue between self and society. For all societies are made up of individuals, and if one refuses to confront one's own inner division, or to admit the private voice, then society will remain static, one-sided, and for the creative imagination, exile will never end.

The theme of resignation and rootlessness is clear in *A Room on the Hill* (1968). The drifting John Lestrade is an intellectual whose sense of guilt binds him to the island from which all he wants is escape. He has seen his best friend Stephen drown and blames himself for his death. He had heard Stephen's cry for help, but had made no immediate effort to respond, paralyzed by the fear of personal involvement, of risking his own chances of survival. The success abroad which his ailing mother had always wished for him, his obligation to escape from the island, had hung like a stone about his neck. With her death, he is *relieved* of ambition, but guilt takes its place. Guilt and the need to pay for what he considers his sin in letting Stephen drown. Ironically, there is a strong suggestion that Stephen's death may have been suicide: "far from being an act of despair," Lestrade realizes, "[it] might have been one of revolt" (p. 119).

Stephen's death takes on a new significance: it forces Lestrade into a recognition of a deeper personal void. "Regret for what his death showed me of myself" (p. 79). What enervates Lestrade, finally, leaving him "like a piece of wood . . . drifting on a wide sea" (p. 101), is his mulatto schizophrenia: "His ancestors, the black ones, were slaves, and his ancestors, the white ones, were their masters" (p. 102).

"Lestrade" is also the name of the mulatto jailer in *Dream on Monkey Mountain* (1972)—Corporal Lestrade "the straddler," torn between crazy old Makak's vision of "Black Consciousness" and his own respect for "White Law," victim of his own racial schizophrenia. Interestingly enough, in *A Room on the Hill*, St. Omer's John Lestrade, seeing the wild, bizarre figure of "Chou Macaque," the familiar black beggar of the town, is "afraid of the giant standing on the pavement" (p. 82). Chou reminds him of something he has denied within himself, but unlike Walcott's Lestrade, he is able to avoid the confrontation. In fact, John Lestrade is not ready for self-discovery. He lacks the courage and the impetus for such a daring enterprise. He takes refuge behind a false persona. Drunk, he sees himself as a clown, a masquerader, ". . . a harlequin wearing the striped clothes that were his symbol" (p. 108). Death seems to follow Lestrade as he attempts to create a false personality out of his own emptiness. Friends die suddenly, and even an acquaintance—a girl he meets at a dance—dies before their arranged second meeting.

Stephenson of "The Lights on the Hill" (Part One of *Shades of Grey*) is also a mulatto—among childhood friends in the country he is "ti-béché" (little white man) but, in town when his urban friends wish to hurt, he is "white nigger." His only accomplishment seems to be his ability to remain disconnected from friends, family, society. A university undergraduate, he has escaped from his own island and from any claim it might have on him. "He was like a man on his annual holiday, in a strange land, unknown." He has no plans, no expectations, no disappointments. But he is in a state of "death-in-life" brought about by his neurotic fear of involvement, and the story begins and ends, significantly, with the shrieking of the inmates from the lunatic asylum on the hill.

The second part of *Shades of Grey*, "Another Time, Another Place," is the story of Derek Charles. We are shown the typical, colonial childhood that was a preparation for self-contempt and exile. And as he watches the city's death by fire, he feels a perverse pleasure in the fact that it will make his going away more logical. Derek wins a scholarship to study abroad and, quite cynically, prepares for his own social emancipation. The white priest/headmaster congratulates him:

"You have a chance," he said, "a unique chance. An opportunity to come back to help . . . your people." Derek smiled. "My people? . . . My children might consider educating their people. I cannot." . . . "Nonsense," [replies the headmaster], "you have an obligation to the boys and girls on this island." His eyes were half closed. Perhaps his Irish nationality made it impossible for him to understand. Or perhaps it was easy, on this island where his cassock made him comfortable, respectable and, above all, secure, for him to play the part of advocate. "Those boys and girls mean nothing whatever to me," Derek said. . . . He had no cause nor any country now other than himself. (pp. 222–23)

Derek has begun the necessary process of individuation from the crowd, from what he sees as "the anonymity" of his forbears. "That black mass that swarmed after Emancipation, dressed in the discarded suits of their former owners . . . without the benefit either of past experience or any vision of future achievement. But he had that vision clearly now" (p. 223).

Derek is the black, working-class West Indian whose education weans him away not only from the social matrix, but from the broken family ties, the sordid poverty of a depressed society, toward a personal vision of success and individual status. Lestrade is the middle-class mulatto whose desire for escape is less justifiable and further complicated by his sense of cultural conflict. Both Derek Charles and John Lestrade seek exile, each self-divided, alienated from a society that offers no scope for personal development. These are the two facets of the inner conflicts which continue to drive the writer and artist into exile, and St. Omer has fittingly combined these two parts of his book to produce *Shades of Grey*. This linking process in St. Omer's novels is incidentally also reflected in the titles. "Another Time, Another Place" (the second part of *Shades of Grey*) gets its title from a quotation in the first part ("The Lights on the Hill"), in which Stephenson dreams he is walking and emerging into "another place, another time." A quote from the first part of *Shades of Grey* provides the title for *Nor Any Country* (1969), where the hero, Peter Breville, a light-brown composite of Derek Charles and John Lestrade, is the intellectual from a working-class family with middle-class aspirations who has traveled to England, got his doctorate, and, after eight years, returned to his native island and the wife he had left behind.

Little has changed. He might never have left the island, as far as his mother is concerned. Progress has been superficial. The town is "a hot, drab imperfectly imitated miniature of a metropolitan shopping centre" (p. 104). With his black friend Colin, successful lawyer and *bon vivant*, a symbol of the new black bourgeoisie, he enjoys a meal of lobster with potatoes, lettuce and tomatoes, all imported from America (as Colin boasts), even the man who cooks it. The colonial attitude dies hard. ". . . A process of copying and imitation, begun on the island's sugar plantations, continued still" (p. 78). Even though "the beach hut and the social club had disappeared, the groups [peasant and elite] were still separate" (p. 77). Society has not really changed, but then neither has Peter. His anonymous existence in England has taught him only that his separateness is real. The image of a bat, blind, flitting about at night, is used to convey the pointlessness of his life in England: like the bats he remembers from his childhood, Peter had

. . . flitted out, sustained by the wings of scholarship and a fear of returning to the island, to bite in libraries at bits of information and, at night, flitted in again to the room he had appropriated temporarily in the alien metropolis. (p. 37)

Phyllis, his wife, had been pregnant when he left home. During his stay abroad she had had twins, now dead: children he had never seen. The futility of a society reluctant to abandon the cast-off clothes of a colonial era, who still insist on a Requiem Mass with bells as a status symbol, disgusts Peter. But society is not entirely to blame for the trauma of Peter's return. There are hints of a personal failing on his part. In an argument with friends in England about the need for roots, it is the white girl friend, Helen, who, ironically, sees the real issue:

"What you want," Helen said, "is a past."

"But we have a past," Colin replied, "there's Africa."

"And Asia and Europe. . . ." Helen smiled. "And you have others as well."

. . . It was then that Colin said, making a joke, "perhaps we are our own past."

"You are," Helen had been serious. "Your past, as a people, shall have only begun with you, now." (p. 79)

It is after this remembered discussion that, later that night, Peter makes love to his estranged but possessive wife, Phyllis, for the first time since his return.

Near the end of the book, the black priest Father Thomas (whose own parents insist on calling him "father") confesses, ironically, to Peter:

"Being a priest seems somehow abortive. I should have been a bridge, like you, a link between our parents and the children you alone will have. . . . I end over the chasm. But you can go to the other side." (p. 101)

This is the final irony, for Peter has failed to find within himself the harmony that will allow him to bridge the chasm between an old, colonial society and the new society that is always stillborn. And in *J-*, *Black Bam and the Masqueraders*, through the story of Peter and Paul, whose names take us back to *Syrop* and the ceremony of initiation into manhood (the Feast of St. Peter and St. Paul), Garth St. Omer focuses more clearly on the central theme of personal emancipation.

The relationship between Peter and his brother Paul, mentioned in *Nor Any Country* only briefly, like Paul's feigned madness, becomes the central theme in *J-, Black Bam and the Masqueraders*. In the former novel, we are given the bare facts of Paul's and Peter's relationships with their women. In a society where illegitimacy is its most shameful, least original sin, marriage becomes more than a ticket to respectability. It is an expiation of guilt. Peter marries Phyllis, the fair-skinned mulatto, because she is pregnant by him and marriage (although Phyllis's light complexion and "good" hair—legacy of a white, promiscuous father—are compensations) is the verdict of a society which, before his exile, he could not afford to refuse. On his return, "the assets of complexion and long hair" have depreciated, and marriage becomes a prison. Paul, on the other hand, had refused to be forced into marriage with the black girl, Patricia, who had become pregnant by him and who later commits suicide. The more accomplished and intellectual of the two brothers, he is also the more courageous individual. The revenge society takes on him is immediate and savage. Denied escape, or even a decent job, he eventually cracks and faces madness.

In *J-, Black Bam and the Masqueraders*, Paul's dilemma and Peter's traumatic return to the prisons of marriage and society are explored in great depth. The sections of the novel are, with one brief exception, all labeled "Paul," "Peter," and "Phyllis" or a combination of these three names. The "triangular barriers" of sin/guilt/punishment again come to mind. Indeed the malignant influence of the past is still very much a present reality, and the boys' father is described almost in terms of the absentee white planter: the benefactor who holds contempt for those he helps. He is a representative of the colonial, layered society:

His remoteness, his stern-ness, like the remoteness and stern-ness of a priest added to his importance . . . and earned for him [a] special respect. (p. 78)

Ironically, he is black, a warder in the jail, an imitation of the stern white godfather image which his society had learned to worship and fear.

And it is such fraudulence that Paul instinctively recognizes, at first imitates, and then tries to confront. Peter, always the less courageous, tries to avoid the confrontation which can lead, not to a genuine reality, but to madness. Phyllis, uneducated, possessive, single-minded in her wish for a child, in a decent if tepid marriage, hurt and puzzled by divisive forces she cannot understand, is a representative of the community at large. These three characters reflect their broken, confused, self-alienated society, and it is out of this chaos that Paul, the outsider, the "madman," sits down (like Naipaul's Ralph Singh in *The Mimic Men*) to attempt to create order, to reassemble the broken parts of his own and of society's schizophrenic role-playing existence.

Paul's tidy, confessional letters to Peter are the central feature of the novel. The calm, orderly prose—at times reminiscent of Ralph Singh's own controlled writing—is deceptive, for the reconstruction of memory that Paul attempts is itself a traumatic return to origins, which can overwhelm. The subtle power of the book comes from the subterranean force of the memories which are visible beneath the calm surface of the writing:

. . . It was, I remember, a Wednesday, St. Mary's College Sports Day, the first Sports Day since I had left school. You had had only a moderate success because you had not trained and I remember being secretly pleased that you would not be proclaimed, as I had been the year before, Victor Ludorum. . . . I received the baton, put my head down, and ran as for my life. I felt as if I had won that race singlehandedly. We went afterwards to the home of one of the runners to share the cake that was the prize. Other Old Boys and some ex-Convent girls joined us. There was liquor and beer and soft drinks. I was speaking to many of the people in that room for the first time. I felt I had begun to arrive, begun to be an Old Boy in the real sense of the word. (pp. 8–9)

Any West Indian over the age of thirty-five will recognize in Paul's anxiety the invidious attributes and symbols of social status or the lack of it, which a colonial-based, middle-class secondary education encouraged.

Paul's self-contempt, accentuated by the rules of a crab-barrel society, gets in the way of his genuine attempt to understand his own emotional confusion. And his acceptance of the role of madman is really a form of self-protection, a masquerade-role through which he confronts and questions his society. His refusal to marry Patsy had not, he later realizes, been merely an assertion of his individuality. It had been a direct confronting of a society that never questioned its own acceptance of an imitative role.

. . . When I confronted Patsy's mother in that dimly-lit bedroom and the scent of soft candle and nutmeg, I forced her to question the role that she played. I replaced her as audience and she had been unable to persuade or explain to me. Or herself. The people she washed for, whose discarded clothes she wore, had always been able to arrange a marriage. I made her, who wore their cast-off clothes, see herself as the cast-off version that she really was of those who had worn them before her. (p. 93)

In the same way, Paul confronts Peter, the other half of his personality from which he had become dissociated. And Peter as we were told in *Nor Any Country* had always felt antagonized, cornered, by Paul's directness. Unlike his brother, Paul had "never liked the masquerade" (p. 30). Peter needs to accept Paul's "coarse, soap-smelling truth"—that one must learn to live with the confusion and pain which results from any confrontation with, or acceptance of, the need for personal integrity in a society that seems to deny it.

This may seem too inconclusive, too vague as a solution to what Walcott, at the end of his preface to *Dream on Monkey Mountain and Other Plays*, calls "the inevitable problem of all island artists: the choice of home or exile, self-realization or spiritual betrayal of one's country" (p. 39), but here, one feels, Walcott's choices are extreme. This is the reaction of a creative mind whose bitterness is in proportion to its greatness. St. Omer's novel ends with Peter, Phyllis, and the baby daughter they now have. Phyllis has never ceased confronting Peter with the fact of the child, which he tries to ignore, but finally learns to accept. She deliberately places the baby where Peter has to see it, gives it to him to hold. He is lying on the bed, Phyllis on one side, the baby in the middle:

The child was crawling over the restricted area on the bed trying, unsuccessfully, to clamber over him. . . . It put a foot in his face, slipped, and would have fallen. But he caught it and held it aloft with both hands, listening to its cries of pleasure, then set it down again in the confining space his body made for it. (p. 92)

The analogy with Peter's own early "imprisonment" in his confining island and society's repression of the individual spirit is quietly but effectively made. Later on one reads that "the child was clambering successfully over the barrier of [Peter's] body and it was pleasurable to feel its weight" (p. 92). One is reminded of Father Thomas's wish that, like Peter, he could be a *bridge* between generations, instead of a dead end, a wall. And though we are not certain whether the child will, in fact, inherit the same walled society which her father has known, the final note of the novel is one of hope.

Peter is alone in his room with the picture of the dead soldier he had cut out from a magazine and pasted on the wall (it is "of a soldier killed in action and lying next to his severed head like a fowl" [p. 92]). The image of a headless body, with its severed head alongside it, takes us full circle back to *Syrop*, and the potential heir of the future, dead on the wharf. It is a startling image, a reminder of Peter's incomplete-ness—his unreadiness (to refer again to *Syrop*) for the initiation into full manhood in the Feast of St. Peter and St. Paul. For he has not come to terms with himself nor with his mad, changed brother. As Peter leaves the room, Phyllis's footsteps are heard following, and the last sound is that of the baby suckling at her breast. The ordinariness of the image contrasts sharply with the bizarre photograph which, for Peter, is symbol of his private *angst*. But it serves as a reminder of what Peter has yet to do. To accept the commonplace, which is life; and by becoming responsible for himself, to discover his responsibil-ity to the confusion and chaos which also is life. Walcott, in a poem dedicated to Garth St. Omer ("Homecoming: Anse La Raye," from *The Gulf*, 1969), mirrors the sense of numbness, of nothingness, that Peter feels on his return:

> You sway, reflecting nothing . . .
> There are no rites
> for those who have returned . . .
> there are homecomings without home.

But St. Omer's vision, though bleaker and more uncompromising, in some ways, even than V. S. Naipaul's, nevertheless shares with Nai-paul, with Walcott, and indeed with all really creative writers, the need to strip away the accretions of self-doubt: to emancipate the self so that a genuine return, a real dialogue, can become truly possible.

CHAPTER 3

A Kind of Homecoming

I *Victor Stafford Reid (b. 1913):*
New Day *(1949)*

LIVING abroad, but quarrying his West Indian sensibility and experience for the subject matter of his art, the "exiled" writer almost inevitably returns to a childhood scenario in order to rediscover a "lost domain." For it is the world of childhood that retains the freshest images and the most deeply imprinted experience of a native landscape of sensibility. The need to look back, to reassess one's childhood from the vantage point of maturity, is related to the writer's wish to establish an authentic basis of experience: to repossess, or reinterpret, a past that seems broken and fragmentary to the adult.

For the New World writer especially, like Mark Twain, with no great indigenous national, literary, or cultural traditions to draw upon, a sense of *national* experience and of the peculiar spirit of place must have seemed urgent. *The Adventures of Huckleberry Finn* (1885) does not only evoke the particular spirit of boyhood; it reflects also "the prototype of the national experience." [1] It is a novel that has contributed to the establishment of an *American* landscape of sensibility. The exploratory, often contradictory nature of the American experience of the New World is perhaps most accurately and memorably reflected in American novels of childhood. Indeed, Hemingway is reported as saying that all modern American literature "comes from one book by Mark Twain called *Huckleberry Finn*." The novel of childhood, from Twain to Kerouac, certainly occupies an important place in American fiction, and it is also an important aspect of West Indian fiction. Both literatures grew from a sense of cultural displacement and the need to "indigenize" experience. Both sought to create a new literary currency out of a traditional inherited coinage, in an attempt to allow for a reality more complex and fragmentary than that of the Old World. For the West Indian writer, the attempt was complicated by a hybrid, colonial condition made damaging by a legacy of a cultural and racial amnesia, the result of slavery. The need was for a reality fluid enough to contain his own polymorphic, heterogeneous identity and to place it within a native landscape of feeling.

This is what George Lamming's *In the Castle of My Skin* (1953) succeeds in doing, and one reason why it has become, like *Huckleberry Finn*, a "national classic." The first overt attempt to write a national novel that could also be a novel of identity, however, was made by Victor Stafford Reid, a Jamaican, with *New Day*.

If Mais's *The Hills Were Joyful Together* (1953) is a microcosm of mid-twentieth-century urban Jamaican slum life, then *New Day* is the macrocosm—the historical and social framework—out of which *Hills* was born. The artistic purpose of *New Day* is the assertion of a whole people's culture and way of life against an imposed, European standard. The purpose of *Hills* is narrower: a claim, from the urban slums of Kingston, for dignity and justice directed toward an indifferent, neo-colonial bourgeoisie. *New Day*, beginning with Paul Bogle and the rebellion at Morant Bay in 1865 and ending with Garth Campbell and the promise of internal self-government in 1944, is a largely imaginative reconstruction of the social and historical realities which shaped the identity of modern Jamaica. And if there are disparities between Reid's account of the Morant Bay rebellion (and its repercussions) and the accounts of historians,[2] then such differences are explicable in terms of the different demands of history and fiction, and of Reid's view of what it means to be a Jamaican. For the novel is above all a powerful assertion of a genuinely felt experience: it powerfully reflects a landscape of real feeling, and therefore is an important landmark in the development of the Caribbean sensibility. It is the first West Indian novel written entirely in dialect form and, appropriately enough, is experienced by the reader directly through the eyes of a young boy, Johnny Campbell. The entire novel is concerned with the recollection of the ageing John Campbell (on the eve of the New Constitution of 1944) of his childhood as the youngest member of the middle-class, near-white planter family out of which (as in the case of the Manley family) Jamaica's most famous leaders have come. But *New Day* is not mere "emotion recollected in tranquility": all the senses are evoked to present Johnny's childhood world as a *lived* experience. The use of natural imagery and metaphor, of a dialect-construction of strong, actively physical verbs, a vernacular syntax, contribute to the reality of the world of the novel. Johnny Campbell doesn't sit in the dark, as the book opens, and merely think of the past. He makes his mind "walk back" to the mountains and gulleys of childhood experience:

It is the year 1865. June and July and August gone, and no rain comes with October. Brown on our yam-vines, the earth a-crack with dryness, there is no *osnaburg* to make clothing for our backs, four hundred thousand are a-moan. God O!—there are tears all over the land and only the rich laugh deep. (p. 8)[3]

So the "flashback" begins, and soon one is experiencing the events of the novel as much through the reactions of young Johnny Campbell as through their recounting by the aged narrator. Reid is therefore able to evoke experience while describing events in the development of the story. An example of this is seen when Pa Campbell, at prayer-time, is angry because Davie has disregarded his injunction and gone secretly to hear Paul Bogle speak at Stoney Gut. The reader sees the father's anger and the son's rebelliousness through young Johnny's awed, but incomplete view:

Father is talking again. I see Davie's mouth being stubborn like Custos's mule. My father took the trace-leather in his hand; coconut tree a tremble in March wind is my father now. . . . Barrack-cart going to market on Saturday—day sometimes has no grease on the axle, and that time, the iron rubs on mahoe wood and so is Father's voice. (p. 13)

Reid's frequent use of the extended (almost Virgilian) simile has the effect of filling out the wider framework of Johnny's experience within which the particular event takes place, so that the reader witnesses the actual event, but is made aware—at the same time—of the outer landscape of Jamaica and the political events which will shape the country's future. To Johnny's ears, the warbling of the birds in the trees sounds like "militiamen making skirl with their fifes at Morant Bay when they drum down the Jack at sunset." These same militiamen will play a very different role later on at the courthouse, when the Custos reads the riot act, and later still, when the soldiers shoot down Pa Campbell, Johnny hears "pipes . . . a-skirl in his head" (p. 156). In fact, young Johnny's "wandering attention" is cannily used by Reid to direct our sympathies. Davie's description of Bro' Zaccy O'Gilvie as a "black imperialist" seems merely rancorous until one sees him through Johnny's eyes:

I do no' like Bro' Zaccy. Because of his belt and buckle why I do no' like Bro' Zaccy. Black and crusty is his thick belt with great brass buckle what shapes like wild boar's head . . . and whenever we meet and he shakes my hand, my eyes only reach as high as his belt and I smell the stinking leather. (pp. 44–45)

The young boy's physical revulsion, the child's-eye view of details of Zaccy's dress—like the "black alpaca suit with heavy silver chain *riding* his stomach"—convey much more clearly than Davie's political distaste, the self-concern and greed of Bro' Zaccy, head butcher, vestryman, and traitor. The sinister, untrustworthy nature of Bro' Zaccy is conveyed far more effectively through young Johnny's "random" observations, than by direct comment:

I do no' like Bro' Zaccy in lantern light. Valleys and ridges are there in his face which you do not see in the daytime. He has got his fingers over his eyes, but there is a gleam shining through his fingers, and the gleam is shining on me. I do no' like him in lantern light. (p. 85)

Closely observed physical details are used throughout the novel, to create sensuous links between the boy's private experience and the larger framework of politics and society. So Johnny's feeling, as he watches his father slowly buttoning up his blue frock-coat, that each of the seven brass buttons "was one of us pickneys" (p. 30), provides both a sensitive insight into the Campbell family–relationship, and a measure of structural continuity. Later in the novel, after the rebellion has been cruelly put down and Davie has founded a community off the coast at Salt Savannah Cory, Dr. Geary arrives with a gift. It is Pa Campbell's old brass-buttoned frock coat with the bullet holes sewn up. When Davie puts the coat on he becomes the new Campbell "leader-bull."

The use of natural (mainly animal) imagery keeps the physical level of experience uppermost in the book without forfeiting the political and social relevance of the events recorded. The wild-boar hunt is one such episode. The naturalness of the huntsmen's good spirits after a successful, if exhausting, hunt; the relish with which they fall upon rum and then the pepperpot soup at Miss Martha's Tavern, are kept within the bounds of rural propriety. When Davie and the men leave the tavern nobody can tell that they had been drinking heavily; "quiet talk, straight walk, everybody standing good" (p. 109). Johnny's discovery at the tavern, that "all songs do no'

bring the same contentment" (p. 108), turns out to be more than a
reference to his first tasting of the fiery pepperpot soup. For the
men's feast at the tavern is contrasted with the immoral banqueting
of Custos Von Aldenburg:

> . . . I have heard about whole hogs with pimento and fresh mint packing
> their insides with sweet scents . . . great white yams . . . powdering as
> they reach your tongue; roasted yellow hearts o' breadfruit tasting like
> goats'-milk butter; booby eyes from Morant Cays boiled hard with salt
> and pepper; . . . stewed mango chutney served on kingfish caught on the
> californian banks. . . . (p. 105)

This mouth-watering catalogue has nothing to do with simple contentment; it is gluttony of an inflammatory kind, given the fact that
the poor people are virtually starving; and it is this selfish disregard
for the common suffering that leads to the Custos's death and the riot
which the governor quells with brutal swiftness. The riot itself, seen
through Johnny's eyes, is more vividly conveyed because one shares
his limited perspective. One is forced, as it were, to witness events
from within the crowd, able only to pick out sharp, immediate details:

> I am lying on the ground in the square and a dead man is on me. I see
> the blood a-pour out of the hole in his face. . . . I am watching the
> blood on the ground, coming, coming, a-come closer to me, a long red
> snake. . . . Ha' you heard o' the woman who hugged musket ball to her
> breast, then went slowly to her knees, so that long afterwards thought, we
> thought she was a-pray? (pp. 115–16)

To Johnny's terrified eyes the men who have rushed the courthouse
militia and councilmen are visible only from their shoulders upwards.
Their movements seem to suggest ploughing: "presently . . . the
shoulders move away. I can see they had been ploughing at death" (p.
116). The image of the boar-hunt returns when Deacon Paul Bogle
seeks the "fat German pig," Custos Von Aldenburg: "Deacon is a
hunter-dog quartering the hole o' the German boar" (p. 12). The killing of the fat Custos is not only a "natural" act, however, like the
hunting of the boar, but it is also seen to be an act of righteous retri-
bution that recalls Bogle's real function as a respected, religious
leader of the Stoney Gut people: "Deacon is a cult shepherd in Yal-
lahs Valley waiting for the sacrificial lamb" (p. 127).

Developments of the plot of *New Day* are continually framed

within events and experiences which are rooted in the land, the culture and traditions of a people. The Campbell family are like
Mittelholzer's van Groenwegels of the Kaywana trilogy, a hardy, energetic clan, fiercely loyal to a violent land. But a weak, bourgeois
element is introduced by James Creary, Davie's son by Lucille
Dubois, who marries an English wife and allows his son, Garth, to be
brought up in a superficial, middle-class, un-Campbell-like way.
Reid reestablishes the link between generations by using another
natural symbol: old Pa John's gift to the baby of a traditional red,
jancra bead necklace with a dried cashew-nut on the end. Garth, the
baby, who is to be the true successor to Davie, is surrounded by barriers, and old Johnny Campbell cannot reach him easily. There is the
opulence of James Creary Campbell's home, the supercilious butler,
a dour nurse who is demonstrably English "cause she sits in the deep
chair like there is no depth to it" (p. 240), and finally "Mistress
James" herself. Garth gets hold of the offending necklace, to his
mother's horror ("it is necromancy!"), but is "rescued" from harm as
old Johnny storms out of the house, insulted and enraged by the
woman's absurd condescension. A plague visits the town, however,
and old John, in desperation, kidnaps Garth to save him from the
quarantine order as well as from his foolishly stubborn parents, who
contract the disease and perish.

The third and final part of *New Day* is concerned with Garth's rise
as the new leader, and it is the weakest part of the book. Reid's wish
to pay homage to Garth Campbell/Norman Manley as political hero
tends to overshadow other concerns.

The emphasis on a sensuously *perceived* reality diminishes and, indeed, the urban, metropolitan-trained Garth (he goes to England and
passes his Bar-finals) is a wily folk hero and "a trickified fellow." He
knows that "I grew up *among* my poor friends, but not *with* them" (p.
252). He is another Davie, perhaps, but Cambridge educated and
wearing English tweeds. At the end of the book, it is almost as if a
case has to be made out by Pa John for Garth's rural pedigree.

Hear me. He has come down from a man who had the strength o'ten, a
man who was a mighty boar-hunter. His grand is a man who walked the
Blue Mountains, and birds could no' know when he passed. (p. 338)

The pace and urgency of parts one and two, the immediacy of narra-
tion, give way to a more urban pedestrian tone in the final part. As
Johnny "grows old" and becomes advocate for Garth, his credibility

as observer diminishes. The rootedness of rural life gives way to the more important demands of clever politics; and Garth (unlike Mais's Jake) is an urbane hero who does not hesitate to use his Cambridge and Gray's Inn training in his role as leader of the Folk. There can be no blacksmith's shop for Garth Campbell: his claim to leadership lies through the devious corridors of politics. Standard English also gains precedence over the dialect form, and even Pa John's use of the vernacular often has a forced fabricated quality.

> Nothing to do now but wait and watch. When day-cloud reaches pointer-dog in bird-swamp and he is waiting for ploves to rise, he can do ought but stand steady and keep his eyes clean to see where to point. (p. 269)

New Day, in its epic sweep of eighty years seen through the eyes of Johnny Campbell, manages to be both a discovery and celebration of identity, and a foreshadowing of the growing gulf between rural and urban, folk and bourgeoisie: a gulf that still bedevils the Caribbean, and that helped to create the conditions Mais describes in *The Hills Were Joyful Together* (1953). The distance between Garth Campbell's confident cry of nationhood, "We have proven that race is but skin-shallow and that we are brothers in the depth of us" (p. 138), and Walter Rodney's[4] equally confident disclaimer of Jamaica's racial or political harmony, "The lie is that harmony exists . . . they do not want anybody to challenge their myth about 'Out of Many, One People,' " illustrates important social and cultural differences. It is not simply that one statement is fictional and the other a recorded fact. Garth Campbell is a light-skinned, middle-class political leader; Rodney is a black academic with strong working-class affinities; and for both, Paul Bogle is a revolutionary hero, a black Jamaican patriot. The real gulf is finally not one of race or politics, but of class. Garth's boast that "in our island we have proven that race is skin-shallow" (p. 338) is largely a political expedient, ignoring the deeper division of class which his brother, Davie, who marched with Bogle, had implicitly recognized: "Sympathy for the poor must come from the poor" (p. 195). *New Day* is prophetic of the obdurate division between an urban political and social power and a rural economy, between elite and folk. With Garth, the bond between the Campbells and the land is finally broken. He returns from abroad as a legal engine (as Johnny sees him) on which a "safety valve" has been welded, and his aim is political manipulation of the people for their own good. He is aware that he does not know his own people, and his dedication to their betterment is heavily tinged with personal rhetoric:

They are my people, all of them, regardless of the colour of the skin. We are all Jamaicans—in the sun on high places or in the deep valleys heavy with life! (p. 257)

But true national identity can come only from the genuine (re-) possession of a native landscape of feeling, without which a conflict of loyalties (between urban and rural, self and society, elite and folk) rapidly develops.

Derek Walcott, in his preface to *Dream on Monkey Mountain and Other Plays* (London: Jonathan Cape, 1972), laments the West Indians' lack of this sense of "rootedness":

We have not wholly sunk into our own landscapes, and one gets the feeling at funerals that our bodies make only light, unlasting impressions on our earth . . . the sprout casually stuck in the soil. . . . The migratory West Indian feels rootless on his own earth, chafing at its beaches. (pp. 20–21)

In spite of its primary intention—to celebrate an epic national struggle for independence—*New Day* manages in large measure to convey this rooted sense of identity within a lived landscape. And it is Reid's major achievement.

II   George Lamming's In the Castle of My Skin (1953)

George Lamming's first novel, *In the Castle of My Skin*, is generally regarded, like V. S. Reid's *New Day*, as a "classic" of West Indian fiction. It is one of the earliest novels of any substance to convey, with real assurance, the life of ordinary village folk within a genuinely realized, native landscape: a "peasant novel" (it is Lamming's term) written with deep insight and considerable technical skill. *Castle* is also a partly autobiographical novel of childhood, and, like *New Day*, celebrates the particular feeling of a particular community through the author's ability to recreate the sights, sounds, and even odors of his native Barbados. The assertion of a rooted, indigenous life merges with the theme of a lost, rural innocence to suggest comparison with other, more famous "childhood" novels: with James Joyce's *A Portrait*

of the Artist as a Young Man (1916), for example, where Stephen
Dedalus's love/hate relationship with his native Ireland ends in vol-
untary exile; or with Mark Twain's *The Adventures of Huckleberry
Finn* (1885), that early assertion of American literary independence,
native wit, and lost innocence.

New Day, Huckleberry Finn, and *A Portrait of the Artist* all celebrate, in different ways, "the prototype of the national experience";
but in Lamming's novel there is no such celebration. No sense of a
national consciousness emerges. To Lamming's young hero, G,
Stephen Dedalus's vow "to forge in the smithy of my soul the un-
created conscience of my race" would have sounded remarkably like
arrogance; and Huck Finn's confident, existential *American-ness*
would have seemed impossibly precocious. Nor could he have seen
himself, like Reid's Johnny Campbell, as a member of an illustrious,
proud family. G's ninth birthday, with which the book opens, is a sad
reminder of his own shaky sense of identity:

> My birth began with an almost total absense of family relations . . . and
> loneliness from which had subsequently grown the consolation of freedom
> was the legacy with which my first year opened. (p. 12)[5]

The consciousness which develops is that of the private individual
within the framework of his own little village community. Even *other*
village communities remain largely outside the young G's focus. His
is a gradual, often painful growth toward a personal view of the immediate community: it is a much narrower stage than Reid provides
for his drama of the events of the great 1865 Morant Bay rebellion
(there is, by contrast, only a timid riot in *Castle*), yet the "inner"
action is equally urgent. For Lamming's villagers are acquiescent
colonials whose acceptance of their island as a "Little England" is
uncritical; and it is an acceptance that leaves them without authentic
identity whether they know it or not. When Trumper (recently returned from America) speaks of "his people," G (whose name we
never discover) thinks he means the villagers. "You ain't a thing till
you know it," snorts Trumper, "and that's why you and none o' you
on this island is a negro yet" (pp. 297–98). But Trumper's return and
his conversation with G occur during the last few pages. The idea of
national or racial consciousness as a goal remains peripheral, outside
the range of G's experience.

So, *Castle* does seem closer to a novel like *A Portrait of the Artist
as a Young Man* (or, nearer home, V. S. Naipaul's *Miguel Street*

[1959]) because of its main theme—the development and growth of
the young narrator's sensitive awareness in a repressive island community and his inevitable drift toward alienation and exile. For if, as
Lamming asserts in *The Pleasures of Exile* (1960), "unawareness is
the basic characteristic of the slave," it is also regrettably true that
"awareness" is frequently a guarantee of isolation. As Boy Blue puts
it,

I don't mean that you'll get great, an' don't want to speak to anybody.
. . . I mean you'll get the feeling there ain't no other man like yourself,
that you is you . . . an' that everybody else is different from you. . . .
Boy, you'll get so lonely 'twould be a shame. (p. 143)

And it is finally G's growing conviction of his uniqueness, of "some
infinitely gentle, infinitely suffering thing" *within*, needing protection, that isolates him from others. Near the end of the novel, as he
prepares to leave the island, he writes in his diary:[6]

Tomorrow I leave. The likenesses will meet and make merry, but they
won't know you, the you that's hidden somewhere in the castle of your
skin. (p. 261)

This "you" is the frail inner self, subject to the destructive elements
outside (like the fragile chattel houses frequently carried away by
floods) which G early discovers must be guarded within the "castle,"
for "the season of flood could change everything. The floods could
level the stature and even conceal the identity of the village" (p. 11).
From the novel's opening the activity of the natural elements outside
is seen to be ambiguous. Rain is a blessing and curse, the land a necessary but treacherous possession. Village life is rooted in the land, but
it is a land frequently washed away by flood, the object of human
greed as well as devotion, a land which is finally sold from under the
villagers by black speculators risen from their own ranks. And it is a
land which G must eventually leave.
    G's sensitive nature is first reflected in his childish imaginings as he
lies in bed in the dark, the flood waters rising outside:

I opened my eyes and saw enormous phantoms with eyes of fire and
crowned with bulls' horns stalking through the dark. I closed my eyes and
the phantoms went. . . . My eyes opened and closed, opened/closed
opened/closed opened/closed, but they would not go. (pp. 13–14)

The mocking phantoms that populate his mind are the expression of that unknown, inner world which he must learn to explore and finally to possess. It is a heroic task, given the general fear in the villagers of "being different," of not "belonging," which is illustrated in the stories of Jon and Bambi, both paralyzed by the need to make a personal choice which neither is sufficiently individual to make. Bambi dies of a heart attack, unable to reconcile the two women, the two modes of his life, and Jon ends, literally, up a tree, stunned by the need for an impossible choice, committed to two simultaneous weddings. To G and his friends, who discuss these almost legendary village events, the moral of the stories is clearly the danger of individualism:

A thing go off in yuh head pop pop, an' you's a different man. . . . You start to feel you different from everybody else. . . . You start to believe you see things nobody else see, an' you think things nobody else think, an' that sort of thing can take you far, far, far. . . . You'd be a sort of man on a rock with nobody else standin' near you, although there's plenty other people 'round. . . . That is what could happen if that feelin' of being sort of different go to yuh head. (p. 143)

But it is precisely this feeling of "being sort of different" which G learns to respect and recognize as necessary, if he is to discover "the you that's hidden somewhere in the castle of your skin." Like Joyce's Stephen and like V. S. Naipaul's young narrator in *Miguel Street*, G spends his childhood preparing to fly the nets of social convention, prejudice, and frustration in order to continue to grow and develop as an individual: it is an unconscious preparation for exile.

From the outset, G is shown discovering his essential difference from others, his aloneness within the village community. An early episode, where he stands naked in the yard, observed by the neighbors' children while his mother bathes him, manages to be both a celebration of the community life of the yards and an illustration of G's sense of loneliness within it. The accidentally damaged pumpkin-vine, the anger of Bob's mother, the laughter of the children peeping over the fences all contribute to a sense of a tightly knit, living community. But G, temporarily forgotten in the general hubbub, is left vulnerable:

On all sides the fences had been weighed down with people, boys and girls and grown-ups. The girls were laughing and looking across to where I stood on the pool of pebbles, naked, waiting. . . . The sun had dried me thoroughly, and now it seemed that I had not been bathed, but brought out in open condemnation and placed in the middle of the yard waiting like one crucified to be jeered at. (p. 19)

To the boy's eyes, home-life and village-life still present a whole, if not fully comprehensible, pattern. G thinks:

Miss Foster. My mother. Bob's mother. It seemed they were three pieces in a pattern which remained constant. . . . In the broad savannah where the grass low cropped sang in the singeing heat the pattern had widened. Not three, nor thirteen, but thirty. Perhaps three hundred. Men. Women. Children. The men at cricket. The children at hide and seek. The women laying out their starched clothes to dry. (pp. 24–25)

But the snake in this particular Eden is evident in the very nature of the society's history and construction. The apparent order of Creighton village, with its benevolent Great House on the hill and its feudal system of landlord/overseer/villager and serf where "the obedient lived in the hope that the Great might not be offended" (p. 29), is deceptive, concealing the germ of discontent and violence. The boys, placing their nails on the railway line to be flattened by the train's iron wheels, unknowingly mirror this darker aspect of the tidy pattern of village life:

> Three. Thirteen. Thirty. Boys.
> Three. Thirteen. Thirty. Knives. (p. 31)

Life in the village does, it is true, have its own distinctive character, its shared, communal rituals (like the customary once-a-week gathering at the crossroads for black pudding and souse), its familiar, respected, and notorious figures. And Lamming's description of his Barbadian community (like Dylan Thomas's of his Welsh community in *Under Milkwood*) is closely and lovingly observed:

Now it is night with the moon sprinkling its light on everything. The wood is a thick shroud of leaves asleep, and the sleep like fog conceals those who within the wood must keep awake. The frogs whisper and wait. (p. 32)

But even here there is a suggestion of *blind* rituals, of undirected, spendthrift energies which underlie and vitiate the quality of life:

All the lights go out, leaving the moon leaking a little on the leaves. An old woman trips along the roadside drunk. . . . And suddenly as if compelled by a force outside herself she stoops against a tree letting her urine come down to the roots. Her underclothes drip and the moon sprinkles the light on everything. The dogs shaggy and obscene in their excitement, the human couples gross and warm in frenzied intercourse. The old woman walks along, her head awhirl with the intoxication of nothingness. . . . Life oozes, a thick weight, through her congested carcass. (p. 33)

The boys' education is largely a matter of irrelevant knowledge and impressive but empty ritual. The former is illustrated when Trumper, Boy Blue, and Bob "test" the words of King Canute to the sea (from the Michael John history book: "the book wid B.C. 55 and the Battle of Hastin's") and find them entirely ineffectual in real life; the latter when G's school celebrates Empire Day with full paraphernalia of Union Jacks, paramilitary parades, and a patriotic address by the white school inspector:

We're all subjects and partakers in the great design, the British Empire, and your loyalty to the Empire can be seen in the splendid performance which your school decorations and the discipline of these squads represent. (p. 38)

The obsequious, black headmaster's later beating of the boy who had giggled during his speech about Queen Victoria's wisdom is not, as the other boys instinctively recognize, "what you would call a *natural* beating" (p. 44). His fury represents an equal and opposite displacement of *angst*, for his public behavior is the result of private frustrations. His status as a black colonial gentleman is precarious: any sudden deflation of self-respect is therefore intolerable. But the beating is particularly savage because he recognizes the boy as the son of his cook who has been a witness to his own humiliation at the hands of his wife.

The boys' experience and tentative discussion of such events lead, especially in G's case, to a gradual development of critical awareness and the need to choose. G's mother flogs him for playing on the corner frequented by "low" types in an attempt to dissuade him from the wrong choice of friends: the policeman, black symbol of white authority, breaks up a village fight with the words: "Why all you can't live like the people in Belleville?" (p. 106). Even the book's natural imagery underlines social and class distinctions:

Only the doves seemed to have found some peace in these surroundings. . . . Neither the sparrows nor the blackbirds making their noise
from the trees flew down to join them, and suddenly it occurred to me
that in the village the sparrows and the blackbirds which were the com-
monest victims of our snares had seldom been joined by the doves. (pp.
110–11)

Belleville, where the white people live, is the home of the doves; the
sparrows and blackbirds live in the village. But the widening pattern
of G's experience makes a choice of sides more and more difficult.
The words he sees in the shapes of clouds, "ARE YOU NOT A
BROTHER?" prefigure his enforced attendance of a revivalist meeting (he, Trumper, and Boy Blue are avoiding pursuit by the white
overseer), where the black preacher also holds out a choice. As the
boys come forward to the table to "witness," but in reality to escape
the overseer, they also (but only implicitly) identify with their peasant roots: the "choice of life" is not to be so easy, for the real threat to
village life comes from within. It is Mr. Slime, ex-teacher, adulterer,
village spokesman, and founder of the Penny Bank and Friendly Society, who eventually betrays his own people when the land speculators begin to operate under his direction. Even old Pa, the respected
village patriarch, gets a notice to quit and is forced to go to the Alms
House to die. Dispossession takes on a symbolic meaning. As Mr. Foster observes: "A man ain't a man till he can call the house he live in
'my own.' " In *Castle*, as in Naipaul's *A House for Mr. Biswas* (1961),
the house represents the individual's personality, the beleaguered inner self which needs to be preserved from destructive forces outside.
     The recurring image of the crabs is a constant reminder of this
need to protect the identity. To G the crabs appear puzzling, self-
contained, their delicate stalklike eyes acting as independent agents
of the creature hidden away within its shell. The schoolboy jingle, "a
b ab catch a crab," gains in significance when we discover that crab-
catching,[7] for the boys, is really a means of self-expression, a personal
accomplishment. The crabs they try to catch are not the large,
clumsy (though edible) ones that blunder into the village after heavy
rain, but the small, "decorous" beach-crabs ("like cups and saucers
which my mother bought and *put away*," p. 149, my italics). "Boy
Blue didn't really want to eat one of these. He wanted to catch them
as a kind of triumph" (p. 150). The hesitant, secretive movements of
the crabs act as a kind of counterpoint to the stories of Bambi and

Jon, both of which illustrate the theme of the beleaguered self and the dangers of premature individuation. Bambi's tragedy comes not as the result of his inability to choose between Bots and Bambina, but because he cannot satisfy a social convention which is alien to his private experience. His decision to marry one of the women (to mollify a well-meaning "white woman," a social reformer) sets up an internal conflict which he is powerless to understand or control. He suffers an emotional split, and (like Jon-up-the-tree)[8] his personality eventually falls apart. Jon is also insufficiently "individuated" to distinguish between a logical and a psychological truth:

> "That would make it that there was two Jons," Boy Blue said, "one in the tree an' one in the church, whichever church he did choose."
> P'raps three Jons," Trumper said. . . . "Three Jons," Boy Blue repeated, "one in the tree, an' one in each church. But it don't make sense. . . . It ain't what the teacher does call logical." (p. 131)

G soon learns that the inner "you" is fragile, unknown, and complex; and that its growth is not only a hesitant, crablike movement toward "awareness," toward real freedom of choice, but also a process hedged about with dangers against which it must be protected, like the tender crab within its "castle" of shell. The pebble which he finds one day on the top of a heap of others "as though it *stood out from the others* and asked to be taken away" (p. 214, my italics), soon takes on a symbolic meaning for him. It is no longer a pebble, but the *lapis* of his inner self, his individuality; and his first impulse is to protect, to *hide* it from others. Its subsequent, mysterious disappearance crystallizes G's growing sense of loss, of alienation from home and village. It is the beginning of exile.

For G has the questing, sensitive awareness of the creative artist, and in his development the natural, undifferentiated world of the village and the private world of literature and art inevitably draw apart. His overriding concern becomes a need to preserve this new sense of integrity as a private individual in a society that can no longer nourish or contain him. But if G—a high-school product now—can no longer find acceptance with the villagers, it is also true to say that he cannot relate meaningfully to his new status:

If I asserted myself they made it clear that I didn't belong just as Bob, Trumper and Boy Blue later insisted that I was no longer one of the boys. Whether or not they wanted to they excluded me from their world just as my memory of them and the village excluded me from the world of the High School. (p. 220)

Yet G recognizes that the reason for his sense of alienation is some-thing more than the high school. It is that sensitive, inner thing within the castle of his skin that has made the difference. The gulf was always waiting. At the end of the book he says:

When I review these relationships they seem so odd. I have always been here on this side and the other person there on that side, and we have both tried to make the sides appear similar in needs, desires and ambi-tions. But it wasn't true. It was never true. (p. 261)

Emigration, exile, is the next step. But it was always an inevitable, a *necessary* exile.

CHAPTER 4

New Directions:
From W. Hudson's Green Mansions
to W. Harris's Cultivated Wilderness

I   W. H. Hudson (1841–1922)

SUBTITLED "A Romance of the Tropical Forest," *Green Mansions*[1] is the fictional biography of Abel Guevez de Argensola (called "Mr. Abel" throughout the book), a Venezuelan intellectual and political exile living in Georgetown, British Guiana, in the late nineteenth century. The narrator becomes his intimate friend and learns of Mr. Abel's extraordinary journey, on foot, from Venezuela to Guiana twelve years previously. The novel is a recounting of that journey, of Abel's encounters with certain "savage" tribes of Amerindians and, above all, of his love for the mysterious forest girl, Rima.

Abel's journey begins as an attempt to escape from Venezuela. He is implicated in a coup that misfires. Once south of the Orinoco River, however, he is drawn to the great, unexplored rain forest of the interior, and decides to indulge a childhood dream "to visit this primitive wilderness" (p. 9). Hudson was a gifted naturalist with an observant eye for all that was interesting or strange in the world of experience. Not surprisingly, therefore, Mr. Abel, who is in many ways a projection of the author, sets out for the interior intending to record in his journal all the information he can gather about the "savage" tribes and the flora and fauna of the region. After six months of these "wanderings," however, he falls ill and his journal is ruined by rain, the manuscript reduced to a sodden pulp. He is looked after by a rough Venezuelan trader, Don Panta, who (like some spiritual guide) sends him deeper into the interior in the company of a tribe of mountain-dwelling Indians. Abel himself sees Panta as "a kind of savage beast that had sprung on me, not to rend, but to rescue from death" (p.

14).[2] Abel's journey develops spiritual overtones, and Panta and the "savage" Indians appear to act "like passive agents of some higher power" (p. 14).

Abel next discovers a gold necklace worn by one of the Indians and succumbs to a European gold-lust: "the old dream of gold . . . that has drawn so many minds since the days of Alonzo Pizarro" (p. 21). Inflamed by the thought of fabulous wealth, he searches for an "El Dorado" for weeks without success. The beauty and strangeness of the landscape exert, however, an unconsciously calming effect on him. He begins to notice a change within: the explorer becomes aware of the unknown territory of himself.

This unexpected peace which I had found now seemed to me of infinitely greater value than that yellow metal I had missed finding. . . . (p. 21)

It is "a blessed disillusionment" and marks the second stage of his journey:

This was the end of my second period in Guayana; the first had been filled with that dream of a book to win me fame . . . the second . . . with the dream of boundless wealth. . . . (p. 21)

Abel's frank hatred of the "savage" mind begins to give way to his need for temporary acceptance in their world. He is nevertheless at pains to uphold the stereotype: he admits to their friendliness and to the good treatment he receives at their hands, but refuses to see them as more than "beasts of prey, plus a cunning or low kind of intelligence" (p. 17). After a drinking bout during which his host, the chief, Runi, welcomes him as a member of the family, Abel, himself intoxicated, declares his friendship and is warmly embraced by Runi. Abel submits and is accepted, but not without "some disagreeable sensations and a pang or two of self-disgust" (p. 27) the next morning.

The Indians, in fact, now become more than vaguely observed "savages." Individuals stand out, like Piaké and his brother, Kua-Ko, and Runi's old mother, the community's storyteller and respected matriarch. And it is at this point, where Abel has at least partially identified with his surroundings and with his "savage" hosts, that he comes upon a thick patch of forest, away from the savannah where the Indians live, the "wild paradise" where he is to meet Rima for the first time. Hudson's description of the rain-forest is remarkably accurate and effective:[3]

Far above me, but not nearly so far as it seemed, the tender gloom of one such chamber or space is traversed now by a golden shaft of light falling through some break in the upper foliage . . . and . . . suspended on nothing to the eye, the shaft reveals a tangle of shining silver threads—the web of some large tree-spider. (p. 33)

It is a rich hunting ground, teeming with animal life and especially with birds, but one which the Indians fear and avoid. The attraction of the place increases for Abel, however, and one day he has a strange experience there. Above the birdsong, he hears a mysterious and beautiful sound, like "a voice purified and brightened to something almost angelic" (p. 38). It is Rima, herself unseen, watching him from the bushes. The key words in Hudson's description of Rima's song are "purified" and "divine." For between the Indians' savannah and the unspoiled paradise of the wood, a conflict of values is built up. The crude life of the "savages" is placed in opposition to the "purity" of the forest, and while Abel needs the material necessities of the Indian community, he craves the ethereal beauty represented by the mysterious, disembodied voice in the forest. Abel quickly realizes that the voice is welcoming to him but not to the Indians. When he is accompanied by Kua-Ko, the forest becomes menacing until the Indian flees and he is alone again.

Finally, Abel sees the owner of the voice. The author's description of Rima is noteworthy for its attempt to convey a picture of beauty at once natural and supernatural, a creature physically attractive yet spiritually pure. He sees in her a "union . . . of two opposite qualities which, with us, cannot or do not exist together" (p. 82). Rima is the representative of a harmony between Nature and Nurture, Savage and Saint. Hudson is clearly anxious to set up his child/woman figure as a convincing symbol of this "wedding" of two opposites; and the tone of the writing appears insistent:

Her hair was . . . loose and abundant . . . but the precise tint was indeterminable, as was that of her skin, which looked neither brown nor white. (p. 66)

Through that unfamiliar lustre of the wild life shone the spiritualising light of mind that made us kin. (p. 83)

But Rima is also an evanescent creature, frequently appearing as an indeterminate, shimmering presence not easily grasped. It is almost as if Hudson, recognizing the essentially abstract nature of his symbolic forest girl, keeps her at arm's length. As Abel reaches out to take hold of her, the pet snake at her feet strikes its fangs into his leg. He runs blindly through the forest and eventually falls unconscious. He survives, however, thanks to Rima, and awakes in the hut of old Nuflo, the girl's guardian, who is also an odd blend of opposing elements.

. . . He was not a pure Indian, for although as brown as old leather, he wore a beard and moustache. A curious face had this old man, which looked as if youth and age had made it a battling ground. . . . His small black eyes were bright and cunning. . . . In this part of his face youth had held its own. . . . But lower down age had conquered. . . . (p. 92)

It is at this point that Abel learns the name of the forest girl, who is in fact the ward of old Nuflo. But Rima, out of the "enchanted forest," is simply a plain, innocent young girl:

Gazing at her countenance, as she stood there silent, shy, and spiritless before me, the image of her brighter self came vividly to my mind, and I could not recover from the astonishment I felt at such a contrast. (p. 97)

Indeed there are, in a sense, two Rimas: the spirit of the forest who epitomizes the blend of a pure and ethereal beauty with wild nature—a Rima of Abel's mind—and the demure, silent young girl, spiritless and dull. When she suddenly assumes her "spirit-self," warbling the mysterious language Abel does not understand, she again becomes evanescent, unknowable. The truth is, Abel cannot himself match the spirituality he admires in the forest girl; and therefore harbors an unconscious wish to possess and dominate her. He knows that he can never "come to her when she called, or respond to her spirit. [To him] they would always be inarticulate sounds . . ." (p. 112). He continually visualizes Rima as a bird to be caught and classified. She is a "mysterious warbler," her hair is like "the glossed plumage of some birds." In the forest she is compared with a humming-bird on the wing and is a "little bird sitting listless in a cage" when she is with her guardian, Nuflo. When Abel, hearing her strange speech die down to a faint, lisping sound, compares it to "the faint note of some small bird falling from a cloud of foliage on the topmost bough of a tree" (p. 113), the image has a dramatic significance. For Rima will meet her death when, trapped in a tall tree by the hated "savages," she falls through the leaves and smoke "like a great white bird" into

the fire beneath. Abel had earlier reacted violently to Kua-Ko's suggestion that he do the tribe a favor by killing with a blow-pipe the
"demon" (as Rima appears to them) of the forest who prevents them
from hunting there. But, in a strange way, he is nevertheless implicated in Rima's death. When he asks Rima to look in his eyes, she
reacts immediately to her fear of being suppressed or "diminished"
by him:

"Oh, I know what I should see there! . . . There is a little black ball in
the middle of your eye; I should see myself in it no bigger than that," and
she marked off about an eighth of her little fingernail. (p. 113)

Hudson was almost certainly unaware of the psychological implications of his hero's relationship with the forest girl as a projection of
his own hidden desire to reconcile "raw" nature and "divine" creation, the sensuous and the refined, flesh and spirit; and one recognizes in Abel's anxieties the dilemma of Hudson the naturalist, reluctantly accepting Darwin's theory of evolution, and Hudson the
religious romantic with a leaning toward mysticism. Again and again
Rima is presented as a "solution" to this dilemma. She is the reconciliation of "savage" and "civilized" ideals, and Hudson elevates her
into an image of perfection.

Why . . . was Rima so much to me? . . . Because nothing so exquisite
had ever been created. All the separate and fragmentary . . . found scattered throughout nature were concentrated and harmoniously combined
in her. (p. 130)

But the image cannot be sustained. It is as if Hudson unconsciously
realized that no static, *fixed* ideal could, in the end, serve to express
the complexity he felt to be at the center of life. As Abel listens to the
beautiful sound of the bell-bird he articulates his author's despair at
solving the dilemma:

O mystic bell-bird . . . ! When the brutish savage and the brutish white
man that slay thee, *one for food, the other for the benefit of science*, shall
have passed away, live still to tell thy message to the blameless spiri-
tualised race that shall come after us. . . . (p. 136, my italics)

The implication of both the Indians and Abel in Rima's death is
clearly prefigured here. Abel, in love now with Rima, is puzzled by
her inexplicable fear of him. When he attempts to touch her, she
avoids him "as if the touch had chilled her warm blood" (p. 131).

Finally, he leaves secretly one night and returns to Runi's village, only to find the place deserted. Alone with his thoughts, Abel comes to realize that he has changed utterly. Civilization, the life in Caracas, had been superficial, and his life in the interior now had become more important:

The old artificial life had not and could not be the real one, in harmony with my deeper and truer nature. (pp. 134–35)

He finds it possible now to forget friends and relations, and even the woman he had loved, "a daughter of civilisation and of the artificial life." [4]

It is at this point in the novel that the most extraordinary development takes place. The ancient, wrinkled Amerindian woman, Cla-cla, appears and she and Abel sit by the fire, talking, smoking, and singing songs. Abel conducts a mock courtship of the old woman, placing passion-flowers in her hair, telling her that she is young and beautiful, and waltzing with her in spite of her delighted screams and struggling. Then he kneels and recites an old song "sung by Mena before Columbus sailed the seas":

> Muy mas clara que la luna
> Sola una
> en el mundo vos nacistes
> tan gentil. . . . (p. 140)

It is the lyric he associates with Rima, and Abel is here making love to Rima via the ancient Cla-cla. It is a remarkable instance of Hudson's unconscious realization that the "divine" forest girl and the "savages" are linked, and that Abel's love for the pure spirit of Rima must take into account the reality of the "savage" Cla-cla. This "reconciliation" is linked with the "inner journey" which Abel is undergoing, a goal which he does not as yet recognize. The next day Abel, longing to see Rima again, sets out for old Nuflo's camp. A storm comes up that night and he loses his way in the dense undergrowth:

I was entombed in thick blackness—blackness of night and cloud and rain and of dripping foliage. . . . I had struggled into a hollow, or hole, as it were. . . . (p. 143)

Rima appears like a guardian angel, a light in the darkness, and guides him to the camp. The episode is symbolic of Abel's need for spiritual guidance, and of the hazards of the "inner journey" he has undertaken. Rima's insistence on going to find Riolama (the home of her lost mother and the mountain range after which she is named) alarms Abel. It is a journey to unknown territory, to "a savage wilderness . . . a blank on the map" (p. 162); but it is Rima's return to her mysterious beginning, to the place where her Madonna-like mother was first seen by Nuflo. In a sense, Rima's journey is the complement of Abel's. She returns to her spiritual home, while Abel must seek to leave his in order to find himself. The novel is full of such juxtapositions, such as the constant parallels of sacred and profane, of "divine" and "savage." Even Rima's religious origin is juxtaposed with the Indians' "profane" version of

the mysterious girl who could not be shot [and] was the offspring of an old man and a Didi who had become enamoured of him; that . . . the Didi had returned to her river, leaving her half-human child to play her malicious pranks on the wood. (p. 219)

And just before Abel undertakes the journey to Riolama, he feels oddly compelled to spend a few days with Runi and the Indians.

He then returns and, with Nuflo and Rima, sets out for Riolama. When they arrive and Rima learns the truth about the extinction of her people and of her mother's death, she is heartbroken but resolute. She has discovered the truth of her origins, recaptured the time of her lost childhood, and recognized in Nuflo's recounting of the past her own fate. Abel offers her his love, but he knows now that he can never possess her nor understand her private language:

So long as she could not commune with me in that better language, which reflected her mind, there would not be that perfect union of soul she so passionately desired. (p. 242)

And it is at this point in the novel that Hudson introduces the legend of the Hata flower: a single white flower which Abel discovers for the first time (p. 234). The Indians believe that only one Hata exists: it blooms in one place for the space of one cycle of the moon. Then it disappears to bloom again in another place, perhaps a distant forest. The changeless beauty of this flower symbolizes Rima's quality of mystic life: ". . . a different kind of life. Unconscious, but higher; perhaps immortal" (p. 234). The incident looks forward to Rima's physical death and rebirth within Abel's mind. She tells him to return to the wood with Nuflo, and determines to go on ahead of them: she must make the return journey alone.

When Abel and Nuflo reach the wood they find the house burned down and Runi and the Indians encamped in the wood. Runi finally tells Abel how they burned Rima in the great tree where she fell "like a great white bird killed with an arrow . . . into the flames beneath" (p. 270). Abel manages to conceal his horror and rage and pretends to go to sleep with the others. He escapes when they are asleep. He is pursued by Kua-Ko, however, and wounded. In the ensuing fight Abel kills the Indian, experiencing "a feeling of savage joy" (p. 274).

Eventually, Abel returns to Runi's camp, secretly gathers up Rima's ashes and places them in an earthen jar. He paints a decoration on it: a pattern of leaves and twining creepers with a serpent wound round the bottom.

Hate-filled, hungry, he becomes almost a savage in his hunt for food, eating lizards, frogs, and even a snake:

I found a serpent coiled up in my way in a small glade, and arming myself with a long stick, I roused him from his siesta, and slew him without mercy. (p. 299)

Abel here is more like the biblical Cain, a murderer. He thinks:

"For were we not . . . , I and the serpent, eaters of the dust singled out and cursed above all cattle? "
    . . . You and I, murderer! You and I, murderer! (pp. 299–300)

At last, Abel is able to accept his reversion to "savagery." He remembers old Nuflo and the wrinkled Cla-cla with sudden affection. For the first time in weeks, he sleeps well. "I tumbled into my straw and slept soundly, animal-like" (p. 306). And as he makes his way back to civilization he is "pursued by phantom savages and pierced by phantom arrows" (p. 310). Indeed, "*the creations of the Indian imagination had now become as real to me as anything in nature*" (p. 310, my italics). He is cured. Abel sees now that savage and sacred exist together as complementary facets of one whole. "For every ravening beast, every cold-blooded venomous thing . . . that shared the forest with her, loved and worshipped Rima" (p. 310). He has become "a new Ahasuerus,[5] cursed by inexpiable crime, yet sustained by a great purpose" (p. 312). He had, in fact, been sustained by his vision of

Rima, for "in those darkest days in the forest I had her as a visitor—a Rima of the mind . . ." (p. 314).

The shaman or medicine-man, the prophet or healer or obeah-man of tribal communities, is a figure of great antiquity. From the Greek seer blind Tiresias through the sixteenth-century prophet Nostradamus to the Mexican Indian spirit-guide Don Juan in the strange novels of Carlos Castaneda, the shaman has always been a key figure in all rites of initiation or *rites de passage.*

Because such initiatory rites (found in all societies) usually deal with a transitional, transformative condition—usually the change from childhood to adulthood—a condition through which not only is knowledge acquired, but a change in Being occurs, the shaman's magical powers of intuition, prophecy, and self-transcendence are, essentially, religious. A *rite de passage* is an attempt to change the innermost nature of the initiate or *neophyte:* an attempt to forge a balanced, integrated identity. It is a process of individuation.

Such rites, in primitive societies, where the secret knowledge of the tribe was conferred on the neophyte, usually involved an imaginative "return to the origins of the world," a recreation of the tribe's history. One modern equivalent of such a "rite" is the psychiatrist's use of hypnosis to allow his disturbed or disoriented patient to drift back into the past, to reconstruct or recover, as it were, his own emotional "history" as a means of regaining mental wholeness.

In primitive societies, however, the *rite de passage* served as an occasion when the myths and legends concerning "the origin of things," the history of the tribe, were communicated to the young neophytes during their isolation after an actual journey through unfamiliar territory—desert or forest, as, for instance, in the "Walkabout" which the Australian Aborigines still practice. The journey was part of their initiation into the awareness of a numinous world: the cosmic nature of existence. For the primitive—and indeed, the medieval man—literal and mythical history (like science and art) were *one.*

Mankind, however, still feels a certain nostalgia for that primitive, cosmic sense of Being. We still feel the need to "open ourselves" to new dimensions of experience: of a time and history that do not deaden or imprison us in a fixed framework of existence. The persistent human wish for self-transcendence through drugs, drink, sex, or science fiction; the now familiar and frequent appearances of self-appointed prophets with revolutionary, religious programs and occasionally with large, but brief followings, are distorted echoes of that primordial sense of the cosmic, the absolute reality of life which was (and is) the object of the shamanistic journey of initiation. And it is in that context that one needs to place the remarkable phenomenon of "the journey to the interior," to the unknown, which runs through Caribbean literature.

The journey, quest, or pilgrimage as a vehicle for self-discovery is not a modern phenomenon. The journeys of the ancient Greek heroes Odysseus, Perseus, and the tragic figures of King Oedipus and Pentheus; the journey of the hero in that remarkable medieval poem *Sir Gawain and the Green Knight* (where Gawain, who leaves Camelot to seek the unknown chapel of the Green Knight, is a changed man on his return) all deal with the theme of self-discovery. Indeed, the evolution of the hero myth, as Joseph Henderson notes,

. . . represents our efforts to deal with the problem of growing up, aided by the illusion of an eternal fiction. (in *Man and His Symbols*, ed. C. G. Jung and M. L. Von Franz. London: Aldus Books, 1964, p. 12)

(Notice, incidentally, the modern implications of "illusion" and "fiction" in his reference to myth.)

In modern literature there are many examples of this theme. Marlowe's voyage up the Congo River toward the enigma of Kurtz in Conrad's *Heart of Darkness*, Huckleberry Finn's journey along the dark Mississippi, T. S. Eliot's circular, poetic journey in *The Four Quartets*, where the end of all his exploration is "to arrive where [he] started and know the place for the first time" ("Little Gidding"), Doris Lessing's *Briefing for a Descent into Hell*, where the disoriented hero relives the world's history during his journey through *inner* space: these are all journeys of self-discovery.

What is remarkable and innovative in the way Caribbean writing has treated this theme, however, is the fact that the hero is usually mixed, a racially and/or culturally heterogeneous character whose need to discover himself is fraught with peculiar dangers as well as with unusually fruitful, creative possibilities. For he is a "marginal man," aware of a condition of racial and cultural amnesia, and must undergo a shamanistic initiation—a *rite de passage*—in order to achieve authentic Being. Such a journey is something more than a quest for "roots." For just as the shaman cannot initiate until he has himself undergone initiation, until he has himself made the "journey to the interior"; so the Caribbean writer is involved, to an extraordinary degree, in the "liminal" process about which he writes. As Derek Walcott puts it in his preface to *Dream on Monkey Mountain*:

"For imagination and body to move with original instinct, we must begin again from the bush" (pp. 25–26). And that play is one of the most compassionate and painful expressions of the journey to the interior. It is an initiation into selfhood marked, as always, by three stages: self-contempt, contempt for everything, contempt for nothing.

W. H. Hudson's *Green Mansions*, therefore, by its use of the archetypal framework of the "wandering Jew" within the context of the South American hero's shamanistic experience during his journey through the Venezuela/Guyana rain forest, was a foreshadowing of this important direction in the Caribbean novel. The idea of the disoriented hero who attempts to discover himself through a journey in which, like the neophyte in a *rite de passage*, he is subjected to various "trials," is, for example, the subject of Alejo Carpentier's *Los Pasos Perdidos* (1953), Denis Williams's *Other Leopards* (1963), and Wilson Harris's *Palace of the Peacock* (1960), three of the most remarkable and innovative novels to come out of the Caribbean.

II   *Denis Williams (b. 1923)*

In Williams's *Other Leopards* (1963), the hero is a self-divided man whose very name, Lionel "Lobo" Froad, suggests a duality which makes him feel inauthentic, a "fraud":

It began way back, with those two names: the one on my birth-certificate, on my black-Frank-Sinatra face; and the one I carried like a pregnant load waiting to be freed. . . . All along, ever since I'd grown up, I'd been Lionel looking for Lobo. I'd felt I ought to become this chap; this *alter ego* of ancestral times that I was sure quietly slumbered behind the cultivated mask. (p. 20)

Froad is a gifted draftsman, working in the Sudan under a white archaeologist called Hughie with whom he has a vital but precarious relationship. Froad admires and respects Hughie's intellectual drive, but resents his frequent suggestions that, as a black man, he ought to be "committed" to his work on black civilizations. Lionel, West Indian negro in an African world, is, in fact, afraid to face the implications of either his West Indian-ness or his African-ness. At the Meriotic Institute, looking at the gold figurine of the African Queen Amanishakete, Froad is reminded of the African woman, Eve, to whom he is strongly attracted:

I knew that this image of Eve, this persistent female, would never leave me as long as I lived. And I resented this. . . . Lobo spoke: this is your woman. I am a man most profoundly attracted by light-coloured, Copt-coloured, mestizo, West Indian mulatto, women. . . . This queen was bronze: close as the sweat on my skin. Too close; not my thing. (pp. 134–35)

Froad is also attracted to Catherine, Hughie's Welsh secretary, but, torn by his own inability to feel himself an integrated person, authen-tic, he alienates both women, feeling threatened by them both. Hughie, too, is a threat to Froad's sense of identity:

For Hughie knew everything. Facts. Genetics, Moorish doorways, Aztec sculpture. . . . Orphism, Morphism, Anthropomorphism, everything. You couldn't tell him anything. You had to be wrong. You had to be corrected. (p. 133)

Finally, Froad refuses to go through with a project which Hughie thinks is important, and is pushed toward an emotional breakdown by Hughie's insensitive, self-consciously Caucasian condescension:

"Ideas are simply wasted on people like you: responsibility, *sacredness of time*, that sort of thing. You won't ever cease to be driven." (p. 210)

Ironically, Hughie sees time not as sacred or mythic, but as a precious commodity. Froad wounds him in the neck with a screwdriver. Run-ning away in the desert, discarding his clothing, attempting to elimi-nate all signs of his presence, smearing himself with clay, Froad is, as he thinks:

. . . a man hunting and running; neither *infra* nor *supra*, not equatorial black, not Mediterranean white. Mulatto, you could say, Sudanic mulatto. Looking both ways. Ochre. Semi. Not desert, but not yet sown. (p. 221)

That description of himself journeying through the desert, his naked body caked with mud, closely resembles the condition of limbo, of the transitional state of the neophyte during a rite of initiation. Fi-nally, Froad climbs a tree to be, as he puts it, "free of the earth," looking at the approaching light in the darkness, wondering if it is Hughie's land-rover or the dawn of a new day. His climbing the tree is also a symbolic act, for the tree, as Mircea Eliade notes in his book on shamanism,[6] represents a hollow pillar of light by which the sha-man climbs up to heaven or down to the underworld.

Lionel Froad had seen himself as a free spirit, an Ariel imprisoned by Hughie-as-Prospero. Just before he stabs Hughie, he tries to sing snatches of "Where the Bee Sucks," Ariel's song which, in the play, hints at his freedom. George Lamming has made creative use of the theme of the Caliban/Prospero relationship as a main strand in his writing, and Shakespeare's *The Tempest* is, in fact, essentially an al-chemical play: a play about shamanistic initiation. Hughie, Froad's clear-headed boss, represents the controlling, intellectual censor which needs to be temporarily silenced before the shamanistic jour-ney to real selfhood can begin, and so that introspection may not be paralyzing. Froad has to be free of Hughie and the relentless, clock-time of history that Hughie represents, to find "a condition outside [Hughie's] method" (p. 222).

The apparent impossibility of Froad's wish to be "free of the earth," to be "nothing," is not therefore merely a symptom of the hero's approaching insanity, but a measure of his acceptance of the limitations of pure intellect. It is a denial of the primacy of the ego as well as of the material and technological methods of his white superior, Hughie; a denial of a mental attitude that has always cast doubt on the whole shamanistic enterprise of the "interior journey."

This element of intellectual self-consciousness (as distinct from self-awareness) is also, one feels, partly responsible for the failure of the hero's inner quest in Carpentier's *The Lost Steps*. There is an ele-ment of Romantic narcissism in the hero's minutely observed experi-ences, his careful balancing of "authentic" and "synthetic." Faced with another reality, one that he had never thought existed, Carpentier's hero feels the need to explain and to analyze: to "fix" it. But the Adelantado's city in the jungle ceases to be a positive inte-grated experience in the process. The claims of the outer life "back there" become irresistible. The threnody which forms in his mind, the harmony which, at last, his experience has begun to yield, must be captured, written down, fixed. So the hero begins to find that the need for paper, a pencil, the material attributes of the outer world, reasserts itself. Another return journey has begun, this time to the work-a-day world of outer reality. But disillusionment soon sets in. When he seeks desperately for that opening in the bush to the inner world he has left, the river has risen. The opening has vanished. It is too late.

III   Wilson Harris (b. 1921)

For Wilson Harris, "exile," deliberately sought and accepted, becomes the necessary first step in the development and growth of the
creative imagination. And it is the sense of exploration, of self-
discovery (as part of a dynamic "drama of consciousness") that marks
his work. His early novels, from *Palace of the Peacock* (1960) to
Heartland (1964), deal with this main theme of the spiritual journey
of the hero who has to discover, by trial and error, an "authentic"
existence. In *Palace of the Peacock*, Donne, the leader of a boat crew
on a journey up river in the Guyana interior, is on a quest that has
many significances, the chief of which is the search for illumination or
true selfhood. All the characters die, yet experience a rebirth or
reawakening in the process. Theirs is also a circular journey, like Sir
Gawain's, from outer, encrusted personality to naked, inner self. The
novel ends:

Each of us now held in his arms what he had been forever seeking and
what he had eternally possessed. (p. 152)

Heartland ends with the disoriented hero, Stevenson, lost, following a
blind trail in the bush, but dimly aware that it may lead him toward a
new beginning. Stevenson has to undergo a process of integration of
his two opposing selves—"the Jekyll and Hyde devil" which Da Silva
sees in his name (R. L. Stevenson's *The Strange Case of Dr. Jekyll and
Mr. Hyde*, 1886). His attempt to follow a trail through dense forest to
the depot—"the storehouse of the heartland"—is "a primitive ordeal
of initiation." The story ends:

Stevenson did not know where the road led. He only knew it was there.
(p. 90)

In the later novels, this theme of the journey toward selfhood is
extended to include and emphasize the idea of the imprisoning quality of personality and the positive value of "*identityless-ness*" of a
"liminal" state, as a means toward a genuine re-sensing of the world.
The need for a rejection of preconceptions and biases about social
and political freedom, about history and tradition, becomes para-
mount.

In *Tumatumari* (1968), Prudence, as the prevailing consciousness in the novel—the figure of Mnemosyne, the Greek Muse of Memory (as well as the embodiment of the rootless, historyless, identity-less condition of West Indian society)—makes an imaginative journey back through history through the labyrinth of memory. It is an "adventure into the hinterland of ancestors." An adventure (like that of Hudson's or Carpentier's hero) that develops into a serious and dangerous game. It is a shamanistic rite of Return to Origins.

In a condition of shock, bordering on nervous breakdown, Prudence (who has lost both her child and husband), sitting atop the Tumatumari fall, begins to resense, to reconstruct a hitherto buried community. A buried past. She begins to understand that the outward, conventional facts of her own life, the apparent respectability of family, of Georgetown middle-class society, like the politics of independence, were only a facade: that there was a "brothel of masks" behind her father's image of respectability, just as the life of the people has been run along the lines of a "hit-and-run" policy of political expediency. It had been a game of deceptions in which she had, unwittingly, taken part. The eye that, in her hallucinated condition, she sees forming within the rock of the waterfall, is the sign of her own inner awareness—the release of her true self from the imprisoning rock of preconceptions and biases. She begins to sense the unwritten history of her family: the history of "the West Indies and the Guianas." It is an awakening to genuine, compassionate awareness.

In *Black Marsden* (1972) the hero, Clive Goodrich, sees the landscape of Scotland as inextricably interwoven with that of his native South America: tropical and Mediterranean civilizations merge in spite of contrasts because he himself has gained freedom from his own, imprisoning "I" which tends to "fix" other people, other cultures in static frames like the eye of a camera.

Later still, in *Companions of the Day and Night* (1975) the hero, "Idiot Nameless," is literally without identity, the nameless, archetypal fool. The book is a sequel to *Black Marsden*. Clive Goodrich receives from Marsden a confused collection of manuscripts, sculptures, and paintings—"the Idiot Nameless collection"—the work of an unknown man, a tourist, whose dead body has been found at the base of the Pyramid of the Sun at Teotihuacan in Mexico. The novel is a flashback as Goodrich edits the writings which begin to reveal "doorways through which the Idiot Nameless moved." He gradually enters the Nameless collection and becomes aware of "the mystery of companionship . . . and . . . frightening wisdom" they embody.

"Idiot Nameless" suffers from epilepsy, a falling sickness by virtue of which, like Prudence, he "falls," as it were, through time, through history. Set in Mexico, the novel brings together modern, Christian civilizations and the ancient cultures of Pre-Columbian man, which, seen through the "open consciousness" of Idiot Nameless, begins to reveal new and forgotten links. "Christian" and "pagan," "sacred" and "profane" cease to be fixed labels and become interdependent states: the model for a carved statuette of the Virgin Mary, he discovers, is a young prostitute. The brutal rape and conquest of Mexico in the name of Christianity is seen as an example of stasis, of a concept of Christian love that had become an imprisoning dogma, just as the worship of the gentle god of life, Quetzalcoatl, had become, for the Aztecs, an imprisoning ritual of blood-letting.

Nameless, astonished to find how much he needs to revise his previous view of pre- and post-Christian ages and cultures, is assailed by a shamanistic inner voice: " . . . self contradictory tongues that speak with the voices of saints, devils and angels all rolled into one."

Such an open view of history and culture, the decision to "risk one's neck" in seeking glimpses of "unsuspected proportions" and hidden correspondences through apparently solid, fixed forms and institutions, is, Harris suggests, a necessary prelude to discovering a *true* reality: to "coming abreast of one's own time." It brings, inevitably, a condition of "alone-ness." This is the potentially creative aspect of "exile" which is central to Harris's work and which gives his novels their "universalizing" quality. Helen Lynd, discussing the "search for Significant Wholes" which engages the attention of both science and art, says:

Writers of the last half century have engaged . . . in the hazards involved in the development of symbols, abundant with meaning, which inform the subject with a wealth of treasured experience . . . symbols that carry in themselves the antithetical sense of primal words . . . the richness and versatility that enlarge the possibilities of language and of experience itself. (*On Shame and the Search for Identity.* London: Routledge and Kegan Paul, 1958, p. 245)

Harris's work, because of its syncretic approach to language and to the symbolic meaning of experience, is notoriously "difficult." Concerned more with the symbolic and contradictory—rather than the literal—meaning of language, he has produced a highly innovative novel-form. As he puts it in an interview printed in *Kas-Kas* (Austin: University of Texas, 1972, p. 52):

. . . I view the novel as a kind of infinite canvas, an infinity. By infinity I mean that one is constantly breaking down things in order to sense a *vision through* things. And that applies to characters as well.

This approach to the novel-as-painting, where words are used to suggest—like the brush strokes of the artist—areas of color, light, and shade, and where the writer's purpose is "to break down things in order to sense a vision through things" boldly challenges the conventional narrative form of the novel. Like James Joyce or Virginia Woolf, Harris, in attempting to explore the deeper resources of language and experience, is in fact extending the boundaries of what we call fiction. One frequently gets the impression of an apparent "breakdown" of language in Harris's fiction, of which the following extract is an example:

Victor trained his encrusted eye. Geological and emotional tapestries. Tragedies. Million year old psyche. Curtains of comedy. War paint. Love paint. Black blonde resources. Blonde black milch-cow. Negro. Indian. White. He felt the humiliating burden of possession and dispossession: metallic loves, threadbare loves—uncanny deprivations. (*Ascent to Omai*, 1970, p. 28)

Taken out of context like this, the passage creates an impression similar to that of certain "surrealistic" paintings, and, to some extent, Harris intends to shock the reader. But the "controlled chaos" of the writing is really part of a desire (like that of the early French surrealist painters Andre Breton, Magritte, Chagall, and others) to *dislocate* the fixed, conventional habit of perception: it is a desire related to what Mircea Eliade calls "the destruction of the language of art" which, as he sees it, is a systematic and radical transformation.

Among many modern artists we sense that the "destruction of the plastic language" is only the first phase of a complex process and that the recreation of a New Universe must necessarily follow (*Myth and Reality*. New York: Allen & Unwin, 1964, p. 73). This appears to be Harris's intention. His novels, from *Palace of the Peacock* onward, illustrate the development of a continually expanding sensibility which questions, fragments, and reassembles "reality" in its search for a genuinely new, all-embracing Art: "a theme of a living drama of conception, the conception of the human person rather than the ideology of the broken individual" (Wilson Harris, *Tradition, the Writer and Society*. New Beacon, 1967, p. 27).

Harris's latest work, *Da Silva da Silva's Cultivated Wilderness and Genesis of the Clowns* (1977), carries forward this theme of the "interior journey" with great technical skill and imaginative power. The hero of *Da Silva* is married and lives in a Holland Park flat in Kensington. He is a composite man. Born in Brazil of Spanish, Portuguese, and African stock, orphaned early, he survives cyclone and flood to be adopted by the British Ambassador. Growing up in England with access to his rich benefactor's library, he gradually becomes convinced that his "parentless" condition obliges him to create, to "paint" himself and his world anew. Seeing everything in terms of his art, he discovers new "illuminations" and "unpredictable densities" within the most apparently solid and uniform people and events. As his "canvases" multiply, the range of his awareness widens. Relationships with Jen, with Manya (the model with "a reputation for chaos"), with schoolmistress Kate Robinson, with Legba Cuffey (composite rebel slave leader/West Indian barman/Haitian folk god), gain in complexity. The bare framework of his life becomes a crowded canvas of interlocking past and present lives and events as he "cultivates" the apparently static wildernesses of identity, historical fact, and urban existence.

The nearby Holland House and park serve as a reminder of the interpenetration of past and present: the park itself is reminiscent of the Ur-garden of Eliot's *Four Quartets*:

. . . Ascended the avenue of limes to the statue of Lord Holland. . . . Oaks, birches, chestnuts, cedars. . . . And through a crack in the painted wood on my canvas I see peacocks and cranes. . . .

Fish in the pool there were darting gold, red, silver. A sudden bird flew through the fountain with a human voice. . . . (p. 27)

Da Silva sketches "hidden densities" in Holland Park: the imposing statue of Lord Holland (himself an adopted orphan) looks across exotic woodland, across "Wildernesse" theater risen from ruined "Great House" toward the New Commonwealth Institute, its "Cromwellian helmet" glinting in the sun. "A dying Empire, a new-born Commonwealth."

The "exhibition" Da Silva mounts at the Institute reflects his response to the potential for change trapped within the now fixed "institutional tone" of that multi-cultural showpiece. The various cultural horizons that thread his eye as he "paints" his way along the various decks of the Institute merge into a complex landscape shining

with "the glimmering light of a perception of value beyond the quan-
titative mirage of civilization": the beginning of a genuine "homecoming."

Genesis of the Clowns emerges from the brooding recollections of
Frank Wellington who also lives in a London flat. Wellington, a government land surveyor in British Guiana during the 1940s, had settled
in Britain in 1954. One morning in the 1970s he receives an anonymous letter telling him of the death of Hope, the black foreman of a
survey team he had led thirty years ago in the interior. At the same
time a letter from a solicitor in Hope Street, Dunfermline, brings
news of a small inheritance through the death of a relative in
Scotland. Odd indeed, that conjunction of dead Guyanese Hope and
bequest via Scottish Hope Street; but it is only the beginning of a
number of related coincidences and insights which flash like sparks,
from the juxtaposition of those two quite ordinary letters. Wellington's now receptive mind drifts back into the past where he is, once
again, leader and paymaster of his racially mixed crew. As the ghosts
of the men again come forward to the paytable Wellington finds that
his relationship with each has been subtly altered. Their wages (now
a symbolic currency of appraisal) have to be computed afresh and his
role as a leader gains a new complexity.

These novels are complementary explorations of impressive depth
into the "divine comedy" of modern existence. The white blossoms
swirling "in circles and counter-circles" along Holland Villas Road
conjure up the contrary undercurrents of Wellington's river surveys
as well as of Guyanese politics and society (and of societies in general)
where cultural and racial stereotypes continue to follow—like Konrad
Lorenz's "imprinted" geese—the projection of their own pro-
grammed desires. The tentlike Commonwealth Institute of *Da Silva*
reappears as Wellington's fragile tent, the collapse of which, during a
thunderstorm, forces him to question his role as father-figure and colonial "master" of all he surveys through the (ironically) inverting eye
of his theodolite. Both painter and surveyor, the complementary
worlds of Art and Science, recognize the need for a new revolution of
sensibility, a new "circulation of the light" trapped in the body of
canvas or theodolite: the light of a true genesis obscured by the "tragedy of polarized cultures."

This "twin-novel" comes to less than 150 pages, but the controlled
profusion of images and ideas, the tightly interlocking strands of language, provide a characteristic density of meaning:

Something was changing across the years, something dark and new within
the box as it reappeared in his head, in her body.

Winter abortion grew dark, darkness of news around the globe, darkness of death. (*Da Silva*, p. 25)

Even in such a short extract a number of ideas proliferate. Da Silva is
here recalling his meeting with Kate Robinson whom he had earlier
sketched when she appeared on television ("within the box"). Kate
had been to see him about the neglected, five-year-old, illegitimate
son of his model, Manya, to ask him to use his influence on the boy's
behalf. Da Silva's superficial estimate of the formidable, practical
schoolmistress undergoes a change as he remembers how, during that
television discussion on the subject of abortion, Kate, stung by the
Victorian prudishness of one of the panelists, had admitted to having
had an abortion herself. Because of her courageous, though embar-
rassed, admission (a rare enough occurrence on the usual, carefully
"balanced," boring television "discussions"), the whole debate had
come alive and, as it were, illuminated the program (Da Silva himself
had immediately adjusted the "brightness" knob on his set). "Winter
abortion" refers to this television (winter) program as well as to the
general abbreviation (or "abortion") of daylight hours during the
winter. The "darkness of news around the globe" is both the general
retailing (on "the box") of unpleasant world headlines and a reference
to the news of the death of Da Silva's father-in-law in Peru. There are
many such instances in the novel of the apparent coincidence of life
and death, of light and dark motifs. Da Silva, as a painter, is particularly "light-sensitive": light is for him an ever-present and flawless
quality of "immaterial truth." His art is aimed at releasing this hidden light:

"The light's there," he said to himself, "but it's been pushed under, driven
down into the body of each canvas, suppressed, even violated. The independence is there, the capacity to be wholly oneself in the way one reads
each *spirit* that threads its way through hollow conventions of art or politics or science." (p. 38)

The painter's wish to release "the forgotten genie in oneself" leads
him to see *all* experience, historical events, human relationships, cultural and racial attitudes, as "canvases" needing only a scrupulous
"cultivation" or release of the light trapped within a wilderness of

space to reveal the inherent unified and pure form of the work as an *ars combinatoria* in which apparently opposed cultures and civilizations share a common armature, a common wealth and poverty of "immaterial" resources of spirit. "A comedy of empire, a dying empire, a newborn commonwealth" (p. 65).

What is particularly remarkable in *Da Silva* is the further development and assurance of Harris's extraordinary style: his meticulous "layering" technique. At times the novel's language seems not so much written as applied, layer on layer, from the carefully blended colors on a palette. Even Da Silva's simple act of leaving his studio to go for a walk conveys a sense of other, coexistent and subterranean levels of experience:

Da Silva moved to the studio door of carven wood in which the sap of lost gardens stood like a milestone tree that shone with invisible lakes and rivers along which explorers had stumbled into the maps of cities and regions.

He moved into the corridor (that shook almost imperceptibly to another corridor of earth or passage of underground trains) and then through another carved door into the street.

This is the final section of the novel, the hero's homecoming. He is a man emerging into the light of a new awareness, a new universe of compassionate understanding, and the novel's language conveys this with a brilliant controlled lyricism:

The winter sky was still alight with enamelled greens and fires and ice apparently beyond all vestige of fabrication since God's handiwork stood there, like the lost sap of unfathomable milestone tree, painted with ironic tonality in concert with every magical drought of the human senses to look through and beyond themselves. (p. 75)

As Da Silva embraces Jen, his wife, who has just discovered that, after eight barren years, she is pregnant, "he encircled the globe then, a global light whose circulation lay through and beyond fear into unfathomable security" (p. 77)

The epigraph to *Genesis of the Clowns*, taken from Wilhelm's translation of *The Secret of the Golden Flower*, immediately links the two novels within this theme of "the circulation of the light." In fact the final scene in *Da Silva* is reflected here in the quotation from Master Lu Tzu on the development of the "seed pearl" of True Being: "It is as if a man and a woman embraced and a conception took place." This "comedy of light," however, is linked with *Da Silva* in other ways. Like Da Silva, Frank Wellington is a white creole with dark antecedents; a man aware of "interior suns" of old and new worlds which he carries within himself. The tentlike structure of the Commonwealth Institute which Da Silva sees as symbolic of "dying empire, newborn commonwealth," reappears in *Genesis of the Clowns* as Wellington's tent in a survey camp in the Guyana interior. During a thunderstorm the ridge pole[7] snaps under the weight of water collected on the tarpaulin and Wellington narrowly escapes injury. His foreman, Hope, who had put up the tent comes to his rescue offering an excuse that produces unexpected echoes:

"It's the wood," said Hope. ". . . Sometimes it got a kind of breaking spot it hard to detect. Inside, if you know what I mean."

Wellington's uneasy feeling that the man had deliberately endangered his life (at the moment of the accident a crack of thunder had sounded like a rifle shot) disguises his own weak spot, an inner desire to maintain the status quo of leader and led. As the surveyor in charge Wellington is identified with the theodolite (the Amerindian crew member regards this "magical" instrument as the "pole of the sun") which becomes symbolic of his social and sexual authority:

I bent my eyes again to the inverting telescope. The sky turned around and lay under my feet in a brilliant pool of dressed light. (p. 93)

Later, he recalls how he had been drawn to the unconscious sexuality of "Mistress Ada," the common-law wife of a crew member, and how he may have "inverted her, seen her, dressed her, undressed her" in his mind's eye. Held almost in awe by his men, who see him as a godlike figure charting rivers and lands with his scientific instruments, Wellington begins to feel a "Copernican revolution of sentiment" taking place within, where he is no longer the axis or "pole of the sun" around which his Guyanese crew revolves. Like Conrad's Kurtz, he had found himself unaccountably adding marginal doodles in his tidily kept fieldbook as he tried to avoid the implications of this new doubt by applying himself assiduously to his work. The members of his crew, who represent the mixture of races in Guyana, become (like the sketches in the margin of his fieldbook)

. . . the shadow play of a genesis of suns . . . of interior suns around which Wellington now turned whereas before they had turned around him in processional sentiment. (p. 86)

This is the theme conveyed by the book's second epigraph, taken from Stuart Hampshire's essay "A Kind of Materialism" (1972): "In the psychology of the sentiments another Copernican revolution is needed." Even the Abary "creek," which Wellington is surveying, seems to offer mocking confirmation of the reversal of established order. The "creek" (actually a tidal river subject to considerable inflow from the sea) reveals unsuspected, submerged countercurrents when, contrary to expectation (and to the consternation of the Amerindian crew members, who see this almost as a cosmic upheaval), the marker-floats proceed to move *against* the surface flow of the river, propelled by deeper, unseen, tidal currents.

From the window of his London flat, Wellington notices the fallen blossoms swirling in circles above the street:

. . . As I glance along the street the blossom rises into a pit of newspapers blackened at the edges with rumours of rigged elections across the Atlantic sea. . . . Revolution within counter-revolution. . . . (p. 92)

This reference to the contemporary Guyanese political scene, with its "rumours of rigged elections," reflects Harris's continuing concern with what R. D. Laing calls "the politics of experience" which underlies our outward, political behavior. As his "ghost crew" return to the paytable, Wellington begins to discern the particular "imprints" of experience that have conditioned their political responses. Here the novel reflects the complex nature of the historical and political events which have created modern Guyana where East Indian and Negro still live in mutual distrust, each prepared to "cut their black nose to spoil their brown face."

In Guyana, on June 16, 1948, the (predominantly black) police, attempting to break up a four-and-a-half-month-old strike of (mainly East Indian) sugar workers, shot and killed five men at plantation Enmore on the east coast. The resulting protest demonstration and march to Georgetown by the strikers, joined by villagers as they went and led by important Indian politicians of the day, is recorded by former P.P.P. (People's Progressive Party) Prime Minister, Dr. Cheddi Jagan, in his book *The West on Trial* (1966). The event was a watershed in Guyana's political history. In Harris's novel, Wellington's survey camp is situated along the Abary River within reach of the public road to Enmore estate. News of the progress of the strike reaches the men from time to time, and through the reactions of Hope, Wellington's black foreman, and Marti Frederick, the East Indian crew member, Harris indicates the deep-lying origins of the Negro/Indian polarity. The "Enmore Affair" is significant here (a black corporal named, by coincidence, Hope, shoots a striker who turns out to be Marti's father), but there are more subtle factors at work. Hope's character is marked by a suppressed "conservative rebelliousness" which expresses itself as a "tyranny of the emotions," a historically based anxiety, a hangover from early postslavery days when there was a serious sexual imbalance in the population figures and women were at a premium. Enforced sexual competition had meant that "his desires were planted in the quarrels of the flesh, the beauty of the flesh, the enigma of the flesh" (p. 100). He is therefore "imprinted" with the role of "consumer," dreaming of stability and economic plenty, but a victim of the enterprise of others.

Marti Frederick's father, shot down in the Enmore strike, is a figure representing the creolized Hindu (his name was originally Persaud), the "poor man's capitalist" for whom the rigorous accretion of material wealth had become imperative, a hangover of indentureship. His sudden death creates a sense of urgency among his offspring who develop a neurotic obsession with capital at the expense of personal and material comfort. They begin a "collective subsistence upon nothing" as a means of future security. "That," Wellington thinks, "was the genesis of Marti Persaud Frederick and Brothers, Guianese capitalists" (p. 105). The "Enmore Affair," therefore, had served merely to crystallize certain "imprinted" attitudes in both Negro and Indian.

The role of the Guyanese woman also derives from a historical "imprint" which has typecast her as a "fertility goddess," a tyrannical, matriarchal role that nevertheless leaves her as an object of sexual rivalry and a passive begetter of children. Wellington recognizes his own implication in the quarrel between Hope and Moseley Adams over "Mistress Ada." He, too, had "undressed" her with an unconsciously proprietorial eye. The woman, Lucille, he also realizes, had been a kind of sexual prize in whom everyone had "invested." Lucille's husband, watchman of a lonely post above the Kamaria falls, is devoted to his obsession with economic investment and needs to suppress sentiment as the complicating factor in personal relationships. His "oriental inscrutability" in fact hides a deep-seated

fear of her damaging "flame of beauty." Lucille leaves him to become Hope's mistress and the central figure in a *crime passionelle* in
which Hope shoots her lover, a black Trinidadian named (through
another typically Harrisian coincidence) Frank Wellington. Hope
then shoots himself.

The novel ends with the anonymous letter with which
Wellington's "Copernican revolution" had begun. Signed "Yours in
hope, F.W.," the letter completes the "inner dialogue" of the hero: it
is the final ironical note in this extraordinary "comedy of light."

IV   *Conclusion*

If we accept that it is the function of art to show meanings and
significance in a way that argument can never do, we must be prepared to accept what is odd and truthful, rather than what is plain
and self-deceptive. We must look more carefully at the riddling, oral
nature of Caribbean literature: its use of myth, folk-rhythms, and
"proverbial" speech forms; its increasing emphasis on a direct involvement of author and audience in an enactment of the journey to
the unknown: a journey in which meaning is *unraveled* only by a will-
ingness to accommodate contraries. This is the magical reality which
lies behind the fixed perception of history as loss, or as a dualism of
Victor and Victim, Master and Slave, Ruler and Ruled.

Caribbean literature, because of its questing, questioning nature, is
often a "riddling" literature. And the reader-critic is faced with
"problematical" works. The critic's traditional role, therefore, as an
opinionated, knowledgeable prescriber or judge is no longer acceptable: it has always been dubious. The form and content of Caribbean
literature, moving as it is in the direction of the contradictory and
paradoxical, of the unsaid being often more important than the said,
of the cryptic, aphoristic style that often appears recondite, requires
the critic to be continually open, vulnerable to possibilities of meaning and of change. The "call" of the work requires the critic's uncon-
ditional "response" to it. A dialogue then becomes possible in which
the critic must take part in order to become possessed by, rather than
possessing, the meaning of the work.

The relationship of this to the *rite de passage*, where knowledge is
imparted through active participation in the riddling process of shamanistic initiation, is clear. It is also related to other so-called "primitive" concepts: the Bantu idea of Nommo, for example, where the

word, the riddle, contains secret power, or the Yoruba system of Ifa, where the prophets or diviners, the Babalawo, manipulate objects (seeds, shells, and so on) and, more importantly, use memorized verses and riddles as the basis of their art. It is a verbal art whose "literary" value is not as important as its religious meaning.

Caribbean writing, then, is no longer simply caught between two "styles," two competing cultures, but has begun to move in the direction of a paradoxical mixture of the oral and the scribal, a nonlinear yet representational mode. It is a diverse, reticular movement: a complex, experimental, and shamanistic art, an art which must be enacted imaginatively, and one in which both writer and reader are involved. And it is in the riddle of the work that the unraveling of the meaning can take place. More than ever, mankind needs what Nicholas Moseley called "a language of crisis";[8] and because of the complexity of our experience it will not be a language that "confirms or reasons in a straight line." It will be a shamanistic language that works by hints, allusions, and metaphor, an art able to hold opposites together. And its ultimate aim, as Carlos Fuentes puts it, will be

the fusing of the triumphant and the defeated, the clamorous and the silent, the consecrate and the outlawed strains of our plural heritage. (Carifesta Forum)

The "difficulty" of modern West Indian novels like George Lamming's *Natives of My Person* (Longman, 1972) or Wilson Harris's *Companions of the Day and Night* (Faber, 1975) is related to this shamanistic thrust which is not articulated in any immediately accessible or fully determinate form, and therefore appears highly individual and private; but, as Raymond Williams notes in "Literature and Society":

The reality of any corporate culture which is going to persist is that it is continually changing. . . . And in relation to this I think we have to recognize a category that I would call the pre-emergent, where the recognition of new experiences, new possible practices, new relations and possible relations, is apprehended but not yet articulated. Indeed, the emergent literature of a period is the articulation in what often seem very isolated and lonely ways at first, of something which is nevertheless coming into social existence, that which I call pre-emergent. (pp. 36–37 in *Contemporary Approaches to English Studies*, ed. Hilda Schiff, London, 1977)

With the work of writers like George Lamming, Vidia Naipaul, Denis Williams, and Wilson Harris, West Indian fiction has already begun articulating the challenge of the "new relations and possible relations" of its society vis-à-vis the world. It is therefore crucial that the critic (as Terry Eagleton observes in another, but similar, context) be less preoccupied with "symmetry" or with sacrosanct models, for

it is . . . the absences, the silences and hiatuses, in a text which . . . tie it most closely to the history from which it is produced. . . . The text . . . is always unachieved, "decentred," irregular, dispersed, constituted by a conflict and a contradiction of meanings, and a scientific criticism will seek for the principle of this diversity. ("Marxist Literary Criticism" in *Contemporary Approaches to English Studies*, p. 101)

It is in its paradoxical principle of diversity, in its contradictory meanings and complex explorations of experience, that the West Indian novel has attained a significance which is both indigenous and universal.

Notes and References

Introduction

1. Two of the more famous of these were James Anthony Froude and Anthony Trollope. Froude's *The English in the West Indies* was published in London in 1887; Trollope's *The West Indies and the Spanish Main*, in 1859.

2. Quotation from the London 1970 edition, Vol. 11, p. 476.

3. An instructive and interesting contrast to De Lisser's version of the 1865 Morant Bay rebellion is provided by Victor S. Reid's *New Day* (1949), discussed in Chapter 3.

4. See, for example, Ramchand's "The Road to Banana Bottom" in *The West Indian Novel and Its Background* (London, 1970). The novel is referred to as "the first classic of West Indian prose" (p. 259).

Chapter One

1. Subtitled "A Story of Jamaica," it was first serialized and published by the *Gleaner* Company in Jamaica in 1913. All quotations are from the 1914 edition.

2. Interview recorded in *Kas-Kas* (Austin, 1972), p. 33.

3. Published in *Trinidad*, vol. 1, Christmas 1929.

4. *Kas-Kas*, p. 33.

5. All quotations are from the Heinemann, London, 1971 edition.

6. *John O'London's Weekly*, May 1, 1953. Quoted in K. Ramchand's *The West Indian Novel and Its Background* (London, 1970), p. 179.

7. All quotations are from the 1966 Jonathan Cape edition of the three novels.

8. The Rastafarians are a sect originating from the underprivileged black youth in Jamaica. See Nettleford, Augier, and Gordon, *The Rastafarians of Jamaica* (Kingston, 1960), also Joseph Owens, *Dread: The Rastafarians of Jamaica* (Jamaica, 1976).

9. See Edward K. Brathwaite's introduction to the 1974 Heinemann edition of *Brother Man*.

10. Jake's role as blacksmith has symbolic overtones. Among the Dogon of Nigeria, for instance, the blacksmith is an intermediary between life (symbolized by the *air*-blowing bellows used) and death (iron comes from the earth, the region of the dead). The Dogon blacksmith's craft is a

guarded, *hereditary* one: marriage outside of craft-families is not allowed. The blacksmith or craftsman (cf. the Roman Vulcan or the Greek Daedalus) may be also seen as a Prometheus figure, a "stealer of fire."

11. Introduction to *Brother Man*, p. xix.

12. Reprinted in *Public Opinion*, Jamaica, June 10, 1966.

13. Mittelholzer in *A Swarthy Boy* (London, 1963), p.17.

14. First published by Eyre and Spottiswoode, London, 1941. All quotations are from this edition of the novel.

15. Mittelholzer, "A Pleasant Career." This is the unpublished second part of his autobiography of which *A Swarthy Boy* is the first part. In the possession of Mrs. Jacqueline Ives.

16. A species of land-crab.

17. This phrase occurs in Harris's *The Secret Ladder* (London, 1963), p. 16, and also refers to the coastal savannahs, the scene of his second novel, *The Far Journey of Oudin* (London, 1961).

18. The main character in V. S. Naipaul's *A House for Mr. Biswas* (London, 1961).

19. In V. S. Naipaul's *The Mystic Masseur* (London, 1957), Ganesh and his wife, Leela, East Indian peasants newly arrived at middle-class respectability, display the same vulgar benevolence to social inferiors. Even the status symbols are similar: "The deputation sat down carefully on the Morris chairs in the verandah and Ganesh shouted for Leela to bring out some coca-cola [*sic*]" (p. 162).

20. The exploits of "Billy Bunter" and the Boys of "Greyfriars" (the first episode appeared in *The Magnet* [London, 1904]) as well as those found in other British Boys' "Weeklies," were familiar reading among middle-class Guyanese youths of the time.

21. From the transcript of "The Exiled Imagination" a BBC "Caribbean Voices" radio program transmitted on the Overseas Service on June 11, 12, and 14, 1963.

22. From "The West Indian Artist in the Contemporary World," transmitted on "Caribbean Voices," BBC, October 21, 1951.

23. G. Lamming, *The Pleasures of Exile* (London, 1960), p. 41.

24. V. S. Naipaul, *The Middle Passage* (London, 1962), p. 41.

25. E. Mittelholzer, *With a Carib Eye* (London: 1962), p. 41.

26. G. Lamming, "The Negro Writer and His World." From a talk delivered on September 21, 1956, at the first International Conference of Negro Writers and Artists held in Paris. Reprinted in *Presence Africaine*, June/November 1956, p. 329. See also *Caribbean Quarterly*, Mona (Kingston), Jamaica, 1958, p. 111.

27. In *Kyk-Over-Al*, Georgetown, British Guiana, Vol. 3 (December 1946): 8.

28. In *Kyk-Over-Al* 19 (Year-end 1954): 96.

29. "Caribbean Voices." Transmitted on the BBC Overseas Service on January 30, 1949.

30. Mittelholzer, *The Jilkington Drama* (London, 1966), p. 124.

31. *Children of Kaywana* (London, 1952), *The Harrowing of Hubertus* (London, 1954), and *Kaywana Blood* (London, 1958).

32. Herr C. Mittelholzer, a white planter, was actually involved in the 1763 uprising in Guyana (Berbice county) and "was attacked, but resisted, cutting off the hand of one of his assailants with a sabre," according to Edgar Mittelholzer in his foreword to *Children of Kaywana* (London, 1960), p. 5. All quotations are from this edition.

33. Mainly James Rodway's three-volume *History of British Guiana* (Georgetown, 1891, 1893, 1894).

34. In Berbice, the slaves, headed by Cuffy, gained control and issued ultimata to the Dutch governor demanding a partitioning of the county. This, "probably the most disastrous slave revolt that ever occurred in any colony" (James Rodway, *History of British Guiana*, Vol. 1, 1891, p. 174), lasted from February 1763 to April 1764, and irrevocably altered the economic, social, and political life of the colony.

35. Quoted in A. J. Seymour, *The Mittelholzer Memorial Lectures* (Georgetown, Guyana, 1968), p. 15.

36. All quotations are taken from the 1954 edition.

37. After the rebellion is put down, the white instigator is brutally tortured and killed, but Danrab is "strung up" to await his fate, then dropped altogether from the story.

38. The name suggests Hubertus's "Faustian" conflict. Interestingly enough, "Faustina" was the name Goethe gave to one of his mistresses, with whom "For the first time he abandoned himself to physical love fully and unfettered by remorse." See Karl Stern, *The Flight from Woman* (London, 1966), p. 246.

39. The title which Mittelholzer had originally intended to use. In a letter to A. J. Seymour, the author mentions *Kaywana Blood* and says: "The true title, of course, is 'The Old Blood' " (quoted in A. J. Seymour, *The Mittelholzer Memorial Lectures*, p. 28).

40. All quotations are from the 1958 edition.

41. The change to an English name reflects the historical and social situation. The country is now in English hands and Stabroek—the main coastal town, where the Greenfields go to live—is now called "Georgetown."

42. As a child, Mittelholzer was terrified of the family's Negro cook, Elvira, who had a grotesque squint. In *A Swarthy Boy* (1963) he writes: "I could not possibly name a character Elvira in one of my novels unless I depicted her as someone sinister" (p. 22). This is a good example of the phenomenon of psychological "conditioning" which Mittelholzer is here suggesting as the underlying reason for his characters' bizarre perversions.

43. Johann Jakob Bachofen, *Das Mutterrecht* (Stuttgart, 1861).

44. Erich Fromm, *The Crisis of Psychoanalysis* (London, 1971), p. 101.

45. Ibid., pp. 104–105.

46. Ibid., p. 105.

47. *A Swarthy Boy*, p. 126.

48. Denis Williams, *Image and Idea in the Arts of the Guyanas* (Guyana, 1969), p. 13.

Chapter Two

1. Derek Walcott, "Ruins of a Great House," *In a Green Night* (London, 1962), p. 20.

2. In *Black World*, New York, March 1973, pp. 88–89.

3. *Kas-Kas*, p. 18.

4. Ibid., p. 15.

5. Interview in *Black World*, p. 9.

6. Arthur Drayton, "The European Factor in West Indian Literature," *Literary Half-Yearly*, Mysore, 11, no. 1 (1970): 95.

7. From an Interview with Adrian Rowe-Evans in *Transition*, Ghana, 8, no. 40 (December 1971): 50, 57.

8. Ibid., p. 59.

9. Interview with Alex Hamilton in the *Guardian*, October 4, 1972, p. 8.

10. A French-based patois.

Chapter Three

1. Leslie Fielder, *Love and Death in the American Novel* (London, 1970), p. 268.

2. See, for example, Bernard Semmel, *Jamaican Blood and Victorian Conscience* (Boston, 1963), for a discussion of the historical facts relating to the Morant Bay events and the "Governor Eyre Controversy."

3. All quotations are from the Heinemann, London, 1973 edition.

4. Dr. Walter Rodney, Lecturer in History at the Mona, Jamaica, campus of the University of the West Indies, was banned from reentering Jamaica in 1968. The "they" of the quotation refers to the government of Jamaica during that period.

5. All quotations are from the Longman Caribbean edition of *In the Castle of My Skin* (1970).

6. At the end of *A Portrait of the Artist as a Young Man*, Stephen, poised for flight from *his* island, also records his thoughts in a diary.

7. In *A House for Mr. Biswas*, Biswas the rebel, the individualist, is called "crab-catcher" as an insult.

8. Denis Williams's *Other Leopards* (1963) ends with Lionel Froad, faced with an insoluble crisis of identity, climbing a tree in order to escape the agony of decision.

Chapter Four

1. First published in London in 1904, Hudson's novel, though not widely known today, deserves an important place in the early fiction of the Caribbean and the Americas, adumbrating as it does both the symbolic use of the South American rain forest locale and the shamanistic journey that takes place within it. All quotations are from the Dent, London, 1967 edition.

2. An image recalling T. S. Eliot's use of the Rev. Lancelot Andrewes's phrase "Christ the tiger" in his poem "Gerontion" (in *Selected Poems* [London, 1971], p. 31). In Wilson Harris's *The Whole Armour* (1962) the image reappears in the figure of the hero, Cristo, who, dressed in a tiger skin, becomes the embodiment of the community's fear and salvation.

3. The more so since his biographer, Morley Roberts, claims that Hudson knew nothing of the tropical rain-forest: "Never in his life did he come near one and enter into its mysteries" (*W. H. Hudson: A Portrait* [London, 1924], p. 131).

4. In Carpentier's *Los Pasos Perdidos* (The Lost Steps), originally published in Mexico in 1953, the hero also loses interest in his worldly mistress, Mouche, once he is in the rain-forest and has met Rosario, who is identified with the natural environment.

5. The legendary "Wandering Jew," condemned to walk the earth until Christ's second coming.

6. Mircea Eliade, *Shamanism* (London, 1964); see especially pp. 120, 132.

7. See Mircea Eliade's *The Sacred and Profane* (New York, 1959), where the central pole or pillar of the primitive house or tent is related to the mythical *Axis Mundi:* "The sky is conceived as a vast tent supported by a central pillar; the tent pole or the central post of the house is assimilated to the Pillars of the World and is so named" (p. 53).

8. Nicholas Moseley, *Experience and Religion* (London, 1967).

Selected Bibliography

PRIMARY SOURCES

DE LISSER, H. G. *Jane's Career: A Story of Jamaica.* New York: Africana Publ. Corp., 1971; London: Methuen, 1914.
———. *Susan Proud Leigh.* London: Methuen, 1915.
———. *Triumphant Squalitone: A Tropical Extravaganza.* Kingston, Jamaica: The Gleaner Co., Ltd., 1917.
———. *Revenge: A Tale of Old Jamaica.* Kingston, Jamaica: The Gleaner Co., Ltd., 1919.
———. *The White Witch of Rosehall.* London: E. Benn, 1929.
———. *Under the Sun: A Jamaican Comedy.* London: E. Benn, 1937.
———. *Psyche.* London: E. Benn, 1952.
———. *Morgan's Daughter.* London: E. Benn, 1953.
———. *The Cup and the Lip.* London: E. Benn, 1956.
———. *The Arawak Girl.* Kingston, Jamaica: Pioneer Press, 1958.
HARRIS, WILSON. *Palace of the Peacock.* London: Faber & Faber, 1960.
———. *The Far Journey of Oudin.* London: Faber & Faber, 1961.
———. *The Whole Armour.* London: Faber & Faber, 1962.
———. *The Secret Ladder.* London: Faber & Faber, 1963.
———. *Heartland.* London: Faber & Faber, 1964.
———. *The Eye of the Scarecrow.* London: Faber & Faber, 1965.
———. *The Waiting Room.* London: Faber & Faber, 1967.
———. *Tumatumari.* London: Faber & Faber, 1968.
———. *Ascent to Omai.* London: Faber & Faber, 1970.
———. *The Sleepers of Roraima.* London: Faber & Faber, 1970.
———. *The Age of the Rainmakers.* London: Faber & Faber, 1971.
———. *Black Marsden.* London: Faber & Faber. 1972.
———. *Companions of the Day and Night.* London: Faber & Faber, 1975.
———. *Da Silva da Silva's Cultivated Wilderness and Genesis of the Clowns.* London: Faber & Faber, 1977.
———. *The Tree of the Sun.* London: Faber & Faber, 1978.
JAMES, C. L. R. *Minty Alley.* London: Secker & Warburg, 1936.
LAMMING, GEORGE. *In the Castle of My Skin.* London: Michael Joseph, 1953; New York: Collier-Macmillan, 1970.
———. *The Emigrants.* London: Michael Joseph, 1954.
———. *Of Age and Innocence.* London: Michael Joseph, 1958.
———. *Season of Adventure.* London: Michael Joseph, 1960.

————. *Water with Berries*. London: Longman, 1971.

————. *Natives of My Person*. London: Longman, 1972.

MAIS, ROGER. *The Hills Were Joyful Together*. London: Jonathan Cape, 1953.

————. *Brother Man*. London: Jonathan Cape, 1954.

————. *Black Lightning*. London: Jonathan Cape, 1955.

————. *The Three Novels of Roger Mais* [issued as one volume]. London: Jonathan Cape, 1966.

McKay, CLAUDE. *Home to Harlem*. New York: Harper & Brothers, 1928.

————. *Banjo: A Story without a Plot*. New York: Harper & Brothers, 1929.

————. *Gingertown* [stories]. New York: Harper & Brothers, 1932.

————. *Banana Bottom*. New York: Harper & Brothers, 1933.

MITTELHOLZER, EDGAR. *Corentyne Thunder*. London: Secker & Warburg, 1941.

————. *A Morning at the Office*. London: Hogarth Press, 1950.

————. [Also as *A Morning in Trinidad*]. New York: Doubleday, 1950.

————. *Shadows Move among Them*. London: Peter Nevill, 1952.

————. *Children of Kaywana*. London: Secker & Warburg, 1952; New York: John Day, 1952.

————. [Reissued as 2 volumes, *Children of Kaywana and Kaywana Heritage*]. London: Secker & Warburg, 1976.

————. *The Weather in Middenshot*. London: Secker & Warburg, 1952; New York: John Day, 1953.

————. *The Life and Death of Sylvia*. London: Secker & Warburg, 1953; New York: John Day, 1954.

————. *The Harrowing of Hubertus*. London: Secker & Warburg, 1955.

————. [Also as *Hubertus*]. New York: John Day, 1955.

————. [Issued as *Kaywana Stock*]. London: Secker & Warburg, 1959.

————. *The Adding Machine*. Kingston, Jamaica: Pioneer Press, 1954.

————. *My Bones and My Flute*. London: Secker & Warburg, 1955.

————. *Of Trees and the Sea*. London: Secker & Warburg, 1956.

————. *A Tale of Three Places*. London: Secker & Warburg, 1957.

————. *Kaywana Blood*. London: Secker & Warburg, 1958.

————. [Also as *The Old Blood*]. New York: Doubleday, 1958.

————. [Issued abridged as *The Old Blood*]. Greenwich, Conn.: Fawcett, 1959.

————. *The Weather Family*. London: Secker & Warburg, 1958.

————. *The Mad McMullochs* [under pseudonym H. Austin Woodsley]. London: Peter Owen, Ltd., 1959.

————. *A Tinkling in the Twilight*. London: Secker & Warburg, 1959.

————. *Latticed Echoes*. London: Secker & Warburg, 1960.

————. *Eltonsbrody*. London: Secker & Warburg, 1960.

————. *The Piling of Clouds*. London: Putnam & Co., 1961.

————. *Thunder Returning*. London: Secker & Warburg, 1961.

————. *The Wounded and the Worried*. London: Putnam & Co., 1962.

————. *Uncle Paul*. London: McDonald & Co., 1963.

————. *The Aloneness of Mrs. Chatham*. London: Library 33, 1965.

————. *The Jilkington Drama*. London: Abelard-Schumann, Ltd., 1965; New York: Abelard-Schumann, Ltd., 1965.

NAIPAUL, VIDIA S. *The Mystic Masseur*. London: Andre Deutsch, 1957.

————. *The Suffrage of Elvira*. London: Andre Deutsch, 1958.

————. *Miguel Street*. London: Andre Deutsch, 1959.

————. *A House for Mr. Biswas*. London: Andre Deutsch, 1961.

————. *Mr. Stone and the Knights Companion*. London: Andre Deutsch, 1963.

————. *The Mimic Men*. London: Andre Deutsch, 1967.

————. *A Flag on the Island* [stories]. London: Andre Deutsch, 1967.

————. *In a Free State*. London: Andre Deutsch, 1971.

————. *Guerillas*. London: Andre Deutsch, 1975.

REID, V. S. *New Day*. New York: Knopf, 1949.

————. *The Leopard*. London: Heinemann, 1958; New York: Viking Press, 1958; Collier Books, 1971.

————. *Sixty-Five (A Children's Novel)*. London: Longman, 1960.

————. *The Young Warriors*. London: Longman, 1967.

————. *Peter of Mount Ephraim*. Jamaica: Jamaica Institute, 1971.

————. *The Jamaicans*. Jamaica: Jamaica Institute, 1977.

ST. OMER, GARTH. "Syrop" [in *Introduction Two: Stories by New Writers*]. London: Faber & Faber, 1954.

————. *Room on the Hill*. London: Faber & Faber, 1968.

————. *Shades of Grey*. London: Faber & Faber, 1968.

————. *Nor Any Country*. London: Faber & Faber, 1969.

————. *J-, Black Bam and the Masqueraders*. London: Faber & Faber, 1972.

WILLIAMS, DENIS. *Other Leopards*. London: Hutchinson's New Authors, Ltd., 1963.

————. *The Third Temptation*. London: Calder & Boyars, Ltd., 1968.

SECONDARY SOURCES

A. Anthologies (short fiction)

DATHORNE, O. R., ed. *Caribbean Narrative*. London, 1966, 246 pp.

HOWES, BARBARA, ed. *From the Green Antilles*. London, 1967.

LIVINGSTON, JAMES T., ed. *Caribbean Rhythms*. New York, 1974, 379 pp.

RAMCHAND, K. *West Indian Narrative*. London: Nelson, 1966, 266 pp. with illustrations. Extracts from early, "pre-West Indian" and later, West Indian works with a commentary. Useful introductory anthology.

SALKEY, ANDREW, ed. *West Indian Stories*. London, 1960, 246 pp.; New York, 1970, as *Island Voices*.

B. Critical Works

BAUGH, EDWARD, ed. *Critics on Caribbean Literature*. London: Allen & Unwin, 1978, 164 pp. A good introduction to and a careful selection of "the best that has been thought and said" on Caribbean writing. Very valuable collection.

JAMES, LOUIS, ed. *The Islands in Between*. Oxford: Oxford University Press, 1968, 166 pp. with bibliographies and photographs. Collection of essays "by diverse hands" on eight novelists.

MOORE, G., ed. *The Chosen Tongue: English Writing in the Tropical World*. London: Longman, 1969, 222 pp. with bibliographies, illustrations. A reliable, free-wheeling survey of African and West Indian writing. Very useful insights into the effect of landscape and environment upon the writers.

RAMCHAND, KENNETH. *An Introduction to the Study of West Indian Literature*. Nelson Caribbean, 1976, 183 pp. Informative critical discussions of eleven texts.

————. *The West Indian Novel and Its Background*. London: Faber & Faber, 1970, 295 pp. with bibliographies. Valuable critique of the novel in a social and cultural context with some detailed critical account of the work of Mais, Naipaul, and McKay.

WALSH, WILLIAM, ed. *Commonwealth Literature*. Oxford: Oxford University Press, 1973, 150 pp. Brief critical survey of Indian, African, West Indian, Canadian, New Zealand, and Australian literature. Interesting "bird's-eye view" of Commonwealth writing but contains some over-generalization and some unfortunate inaccuracies about West Indian writers. (For example, Derek Walcott's poem "A Careful Passion" appears as 'A *Carefree* Passion' (p. 66) and Wilson Harris is credited with five, instead of eight, novels published between 1960 and 1968.)

Index